Shiping Chen · Jiacai Lai · Liang-Jie Zhang
Editors

Metaverse - METAVERSE 2026

22nd International Conference
Held as Part of the Smart Computing Frontier, SCF 2026
Kuala Lumpur, Malaysia, August 22–25, 2026
Proceedings

Springer

Editors
Shiping Chen
CSIRO Data61 and UNSW
Canberra, TAS, Australia

Jiacai Lai
Peking University
Beijing, China

Liang-Jie Zhang
Shenzhen University
Shenzhen, China

ISSN 0302-9743 ISSN 1611-3349 (electronic)
Lecture Notes in Computer Science
ISBN 978-3-032-36772-3 ISBN 978-3-032-36773-0 (eBook)
https://doi.org/10.1007/978-3-032-36773-0

This Springer imprint is published by the registered company Springer Nature Switzerland AG
The registered company address is: Gewerbestrasse 11, 6330 Cham, Switzerland

Lecture Notes in Computer Science 16963

The series Lecture Notes in Computer Science (LNCS), including its subseries Lecture Notes in Artificial Intelligence (LNAI) and Lecture Notes in Bioinformatics (LNBI), has established itself as a medium for the publication of new developments in computer science and information technology research, teaching, and education.

LNCS enjoys close cooperation with the computer science R & D community, the series counts many renowned academics among its volume editors and paper authors, and collaborates with prestigious societies. Its mission is to serve this international community by providing an invaluable service, mainly focused on the publication of conference and workshop proceedings and postproceedings. LNCS commenced publication in 1973.

Preface

To rapidly respond to the changing economy, the World Congress on Services has been naturally extended to become the International Conference on Metaverse to cover immersive services for all vertical industries and area solutions. With the emergence of Metaverse, current services will be gradually transformed into immersive services that construct digital worlds and connect with physical worlds. Immersive services are the core characteristic of Metaverse.

METAVERSE 2026 was a member of the Smart Computing Frontier (SCF). SCF 2026 had the following 10 collocated service-oriented sister conferences: 2026 International Conference on Web Services (ICWS 2026), 2026 International Conference on Cloud Computing (CLOUD 2026), 2026 International Conference on Services Computing (SCC 2026), 2026 International Conference on Big Data (BigData 2026), 2026 International Conference on AI & Multimodal Services (AIMS 2026), 2026 International Conference on Metaverse (METAVERSE 2026), 2026 International Conference on Internet of Things (ICIOT 2026), 2026 International Conference on Cognitive Computing (ICCC 2026), 2026 International Conference on Edge Computing (EDGE 2026), and 2026 International Conference on Blockchain (ICBC 2026).

This volume presents the accepted papers of the 2026 International Conference on Metaverse (METAVERSE 2026), held in Kuala Lumpur, Malaysia during August 22–25, 2026. For this conference, each paper was single-blind reviewed by three independent members of the International Program Committee. After carefully evaluating their originality and quality, we accepted 7 papers from 11 submissions.

We are pleased to thank the authors whose submissions and participation made this conference possible. We also want to express our thanks to the Organizing Committee and Program Committee members, for their dedication in helping to organize the conference and reviewing the submissions. We owe special thanks to the keynote speakers for their impressive speeches.

Finally, we would like to thank operations team members Jing Zeng, Sheng He, Yishuang Ning, and Zhuolin Mei for their excellent work in organizing this conference. We look forward to your future great contributions as a volunteer, author, and conference participant in the fast-growing worldwide services innovations community.

July 2026

Shiping Chen
Jiacai Lai
Liang-Jie Zhang

Organization

Program Chair

Shiping Chen	CSIRO Data61 & UNSW, Australia

Application and Industry Track Chairs

Jiacai Lai	Peking University (Tianjin Binhai) New Generation Information Technology Research Institute, China
Tiehua Zhang	Tongji University, China

Smart Computing Frontier (SCF 2026)

General Chairs

Ali Arsanjani	Google, USA
Wu Chou	Essenlix Corporation, USA

Coordinating Program Chair

Liang-Jie Zhang	Shenzhen University, China

CFO and International Affairs Chair

Min Luo	Services Society, USA

Operation Committee

Jing Zeng	China Gridcom Co., Ltd., China
Yishuang Ning	Tsinghua University, China

Sheng He	Kingdee International Software Group Co., Ltd., China
Zhuolin Mei	Jiujiang University, China

Steering Committee

Calton Pu (Co-chair)	Georgia Tech, USA
Liang-Jie Zhang (Co-chair)	Shenzhen University, China

METAVERSE 2026 Program Committee

Artem Barger	Idea Blockchain Research Lab, Israel
Changhao Chenli	Indiana Institute of Technology, USA
Ben Falchuk	Peraton Labs, USA
Xinxin Fan	IoTeX, USA
Atheer Alaa Hammad	Shivaji University, India
Avery Hughes	Indiana Institute of Technology, USA
Hasan Ali Khattak	National University of Sciences and Technology, Pakistan
Hailong Liao	University of Chinese Academy of Sciences, China
Stefano Sebastio	Raytheon Technologies, Ireland
Nikhil Singhal	Meta, USA
Rohan Vardhan	Meta (Facebook), USA
Yathish Naraganahalli Veeerabhadraiah	New York University, USA
Pengfei Wang	Dalian University of Technology, China
Santosh Yerasuri	California State University Northridge, USA
Kunjing Zhang	Institute of Computing Technology, CAS, China

Conference Sponsor – Services Society

The Services Society (S2) is a non-profit professional organization that has been created to promote worldwide research and technical collaboration in services innovations among academia and industrial professionals. Its members are volunteers from industry and academia with common interests. S2 is registered in the USA as a "501(c) organization", which means that it is an American tax-exempt nonprofit organization. S2 collaborates with other professional organizations to sponsor or co-sponsor conferences and to promote an effective services curriculum in colleges and universities. S2 initiates and promotes a "Services University" program worldwide to bridge the gap between industrial needs and university instruction.

The Services Sector accounted for 79.5% of the GDP of the USA in 2016. The Services Society has formed 5 Special Interest Groups (SIGs) to support technology- and domain-specific professional activities.

- Special Interest Group on Services Computing (SIG-SC)
- Special Interest Group on Big Data (SIG-BD)
- Special Interest Group on Cloud Computing (SIG-CLOUD)
- Special Interest Group on Artificial Intelligence (SIG-AI)
- Special Interest Group on Metaverse (SIG-Metaverse)

About the Smart Computing Frontier (SCF)

As the founding member of the Services Conference Federation (SCF), now the Smart Computing Frontier, the first **International Conference on Web Services (ICWS)** was held in June 2003 in Las Vegas, USA. Meanwhile, the First International Conference on Web Services - Europe 2003 (ICWS-Europe 2003) was held in Germany in October 2003. ICWS-Europe 2003 was an extended event of the 2003 International Conference on Web Services (ICWS 2003) in Europe. In 2004, ICWS-Europe was changed to the European Conference on Web Services (ECOWS), which was held in Erfurt, Germany.

Sponsored by the Services Society and Springer, SCF 2018 and SCF 2019 were held successfully on June 25 – June 30, 2018, in Seattle, USA, and on June 25 – June 30, 2019, in San Diego, USA. SCF 2020 and SCF 2021 were held successfully online with a satellite session in Shenzhen, China. SCF 2022 and 2023 were held successfully on December 10–14, 2022 and on September 23–26, 2023, in Hawaii, USA. SCF 2024 was held successfully on November 16–19, 2024, in Bangkok, Thailand. SCF 2025 was successfully held on September 25–30, 2025, in Hong Kong, China. To celebrate its 24rd birthday, SCF 2026 was held on August 22–25, 2026, in Kuala Lumpur, Malaysia.

In the past 23 years, the ICWS community has expanded from Web engineering innovations to scientific research for the whole services industry. Service delivery platforms have been expanded to mobile platforms, the Internet of Things, cloud computing, and edge computing. The services ecosystem has gradually been enabled, value-added, and intelligence embedded through enabling technologies such as big data, artificial intelligence, and cognitive computing. In the coming years, all transactions with multiple parties involved will be transformed into blockchain and metaverse.

Based on technology trends and best practices in the field, the Smart Computing Frontier (SCF) will continue serving as the conference umbrella's code name for all services-related conferences. SCF 2026 defined the future of New ABCDE (AI, Blockchain, Cloud, BigData & IOT) and entered the 5G for Services Era. **The theme of SCF 2026 was Agentic AI as a Service (AAIaaS).** We are very proud to announce that SCF 2026's 10 co-located theme topic conferences all centered around "services", with each focusing on exploring different themes (web-based services, cloud-based services, Big Data-based services, services innovation lifecycle, AI-driven ubiquitous services, blockchain-driven trust service ecosystems, industry-specific services and applications, and emerging service-oriented technologies).

- **Bigger Platform:** The 10 collocated conferences (SCF 2026) were sponsored by the Services Society, which is the world-leading not-for-profit organization (501(c)(3)) dedicated to the service of more than 30,000 worldwide Services Computing researchers and practitioners. A bigger platform means bigger opportunities for all volunteers, authors, and participants. Meanwhile, Springer provided sponsorship of the best paper awards and other professional activities. All the 10 conference proceedings of SCF 2026 were published by Springer and indexed in the **ISI Conference Proceedings Citation Index (included in Web of Science), Engineering**

Index EI (Compendex and Inspec databases), DBLP, Google Scholar, IO-Port, MathSciNet, Scopus, and ZBlMath.

- **Brighter Future:** While celebrating the 2026 version of ICWS, SCF 2026 highlighted the International Conference on AI and Multimodal Services (AIMS 2026) to build the fundamental infrastructure for enabling AIGC services ecosystems. It will also lead our community members to create their own brighter future.
- **Better Model:** SCF 2026 continued to leverage the invented Conference Blockchain Model (CBM) to innovate the organizing practices for all the 10 theme conferences. Senior researchers in the field are welcome to submit proposals to serve as CBM Ambassador for an individual conference to start better interactions during your leadership role in organizing future SCF conferences.

We look forward to your great contributions as a volunteer, author, and conference participant as part of the fast-growing worldwide services innovations community. If you would like to contribute to SCF 2026 as a leading volunteer or try the new Conference Blockchain Model, please feel free to contact us to become a conference volunteer. For other queries or questions, please feel free to visit our conference websites and find contact information on SCF 2026.

All the invited talks and paper presentations of SCF 2020, SCF 2021, and SCF 2022 are open to all Services Society community members for free. You can watch all presentations through SCF 365.

Contents

A Federated Learning Framework Using Partial Verification on Blockchain 1
Kousei Okutsu, Taisei Takahashi, and Kazumasa Omote

AI-Verified Blockchain Trust Architecture for Secure, Explainable, and Interoperable Healthcare Systems 17
Salim Aftab and Taha Sajid

Securing Metaverse Blockchain Infrastructure: LLM-Assisted Vulnerability Detection on Solana and Algorand Smart Contracts 30
Anmol Vats

Research on A-Share Quantitative Market Timing Methods Based on SAPPO (Sentiment-Aware Proximal Policy Optimization) 46
Hailong Liao

Cultivating New Quality Productive Forces in Enterprises: An Analysis of the Driving Role of Artificial Intelligence Applications 60
Qintao Yao, Jingwen Liu, and Shaofeng Ren

Trustless Supply Chain System Utilizing Multiple Blockchains 75
Aoi Kadosugi and Kazumasa Omote

A Fiat-Anchored Dual-Rail Triple-Entry Architecture for SSC-Based K-12 Financial Systems 90
Minh Tuan Le, Dat Thanh Pham, and Congdu Nguyen

Author Index 99

A Federated Learning Framework Using Partial Verification on Blockchain

Kousei Okutsu(✉), Taisei Takahashi, and Kazumasa Omote

University of Tsukuba, Tsukuba, Japan
{s2620543,takahashi.taisei.fw}@u.tsukuba.ac.jp, omote@risk.tsukuba.ac.jp

Abstract. Federated learning enables collaborative model training without centralizing local data, but practical deployment requires mechanisms for verifying submitted updates and deterring misconduct. Blockchain and smart contracts can provide transparent records and automated verification; however, full on-chain verification of training updates is impractical for large models because of gas costs. This paper proposes a smart-contract-based component for partial verification of federated learning updates. Each client submits a hash of the entire commitment sequence before the verification positions are determined, and the contract subsequently verifies an inner-product consistency relation for selected disclosed commitments. The implementation realizes a commit-before-challenge workflow and provides an auditable algebraic consistency check. The present evaluation characterizes the gas cost and execution time of this on-chain consistency-checking component on Sepolia.

Keywords: Federated learning · Blockchain · Smart contract · Partial verification

1 Introduction

1.1 Background

In recent years, conventional centralized learning, in which all data are collected in one place for training, has faced limitations because of stricter personal data protection regulations, the increasing confidentiality of data held by companies and organizations, and communication costs and delays caused by large-scale data transfer. In contrast, federated learning has attracted attention because each client keeps its local data and shares only parameters or gradients with a server, thereby enabling distributed data to be used in an integrated manner [10]. Federated learning is advantageous from the perspectives of privacy protection and data sovereignty, and is expected to be used in situations where data are distributed across organizations and devices, such as mobile devices, medical institutions, and financial institutions.

Although federated learning can be operated by a single trusted coordinator, a different trust problem arises when independently administered organizations

S. Chen et al. (Eds.): METAVERSE 2026, LNCS 16963, pp. 1–16, 2027.
https://doi.org/10.1007/978-3-032-36773-0_1

collaborate without accepting one organization as the sole controller of verification records and acceptance decisions. In such a consortium, participants may require a shared record of when an update representation was fixed, when a verification challenge was generated, which rule was executed, and what result was obtained.

In addition, because the aggregator cannot directly confirm whether each update is a legitimate training result, it is difficult to detect and deter malicious attacks such as data poisoning, backdoor attacks, and model poisoning, as well as free-riding and strategic manipulation of updates [6,7].

To address issues related to transparency, tamper resistance, and procedural fairness, frameworks that combine blockchain and smart contracts with federated learning have been proposed [9].

1.2 Operational Scenario

We consider a cross-organizational federated learning scenario in which multiple independently administered participants, such as medical institutions, financial institutions, or collaborating companies, train a shared model while keeping local data within their own organizations. In this setting, the participants may agree on a verification rule, but they may not want a single organization to unilaterally maintain the ordering of submissions, generate verification challenges, decide whether a check was executed correctly, or keep the only record of verification outcomes.

In the intended operation, a blockchain acts as a common execution and audit layer. It records the timing of commitments and challenges, executes the same verification rule for every participant, and makes the results independently auditable by consortium members or external auditors. The role of the ledger is therefore to support procedural accountability in the update-submission process. In a centrally managed deployment with a trusted aggregator, a conventional database and off-chain verification may be sufficient; the proposed use of blockchain is mainly intended for settings where shared auditability and resistance to unilateral record modification are required.

1.3 Motivation and Contributions

If update submissions and verification records are managed on a blockchain, rewards can be distributed according to the recorded training process. However, it is also necessary to verify submitted updates. Although studies have attempted to verify training computation on smart contracts, public blockchains impose gas costs for data storage and computation, which limits their applicability to large-scale or complex training processes [13].

Prior studies [1,4] have explored lightweight approaches to verifiable federated learning, including zero-knowledge-proof-based verification and probabilistic verification based on random linear checks. Partial verification reduces verification cost by verifying only part of the target. However, because the bytecode of a verification contract is public due to the nature of smart contracts, clients may be able to predict which positions are used for verification. The possibility that a client can generate or adjust an update after the verification positions have been determined and disclosed on the smart contract has not been sufficiently examined.

Therefore, this study investigates a lightweight commit-before-challenge workflow for partial verification. A client submits a hash of its entire commitment sequence before the verification positions are determined, after which the contract checks that the disclosed commitments and summary values satisfy an inner-product relation. The contribution of this paper is threefold: (i) a commit-before-challenge workflow for on-chain partial verification, (ii) an inner-product consistency check based on Pedersen commitments, and (iii) an implementation-level cost analysis on Sepolia. The scope and limitations of the verification guarantee are defined in Sect. 2.3 and discussed in Sect. 6.

2 Preliminaries

2.1 Pedersen Commitment

A Pedersen commitment is a commitment scheme that provides hiding and binding properties under the discrete logarithm assumption [5,11]. Given generators G and H, a commitment C to a value v with randomness r is defined as

$$C = vG + rH. \tag{1}$$

When the discrete logarithm of H with respect to G is unknown, the committed value is hidden, and it is computationally difficult to open the same commitment to a different value.

The property used in this study is additive homomorphism. For commitments to multiple values, linear combinations of commitments correspond to commitments to the same linear combinations of the underlying values. This enables a smart contract to verify linear relationships among committed update elements without directly revealing the elements themselves.

2.2 Inner-Product Consistency

Let $\mathbf{v} = (v_0, \dots, v_{n-1})$ be the model update vector and $\boldsymbol{\alpha} = (\alpha_0, \dots, \alpha_{n-1})$ be the verification coefficient vector. Their inner product is

$$\langle \mathbf{v}, \boldsymbol{\alpha} \rangle = \sum_{i=0}^{n-1} \alpha_i v_i. \tag{2}$$

For each update element v_i, the client prepares a Pedersen commitment

$$C_i = v_i G + r_i H. \tag{3}$$

To verify a linear summary of the committed update without revealing each v_i, the verifier considers the same linear combination over the commitments. By substituting Eq. (3) into this linear combination, we obtain

$$\sum_{i=0}^{n-1} \alpha_i C_i = \left(\sum_{i=0}^{n-1} \alpha_i v_i\right) G + \left(\sum_{i=0}^{n-1} \alpha_i r_i\right) H. \tag{4}$$

This equation shows that the linear combination of commitments is itself a Pedersen commitment to the inner product $\sum_{i=0}^{n-1} \alpha_i v_i$, with randomness $\sum_{i=0}^{n-1} \alpha_i r_i$. Therefore, if a client submits summary values

$$t = \sum_{i=0}^{n-1} \alpha_i v_i, \qquad \rho = \sum_{i=0}^{n-1} \alpha_i r_i, \tag{5}$$

a verifier can check whether

$$\sum_{i=0}^{n-1} \alpha_i C_i = tG + \rho H \tag{6}$$

holds. In this study, this property is used to verify the consistency between selected committed update elements and the submitted summary values on a smart contract, without revealing each update element.

2.3 Terminology and Verification Scope

Post-selection update manipulation denotes behavior in which a client constructs or modifies an update representation, disclosed elements, or summary values after learning the verification challenge so that only the challenged relation is satisfied. *Prior binding* denotes fixing a representation of the full update before that challenge is determined. In the present implementation, prior binding is represented by a hash of the full commitment sequence.

Algebraic consistency means that the disclosed commitments and submitted summary values satisfy the prescribed inner-product relation. This property is conditional on the disclosed commitments and does not imply correct local training, semantic validity, data quality, freshness, originality, or usefulness of an update. *Element-level correspondence* means that every disclosed commitment is proven to occupy the claimed position in the previously bound full commitment sequence. The current implementation does not provide element-level correspondence.

3 Related Work

3.1 Discussion on zk-SNARKs

Ebrahimi et al. [4] proposed a framework that combines zero-knowledge proofs and blockchain to make local training and global aggregation in federated learning verifiable. In their framework, clients generate zk-SNARK-based proofs showing that they executed local training using the global model shared on-chain and that the resulting local model is consistent with the computation. The aggregator also generates a proof showing that aggregation was performed only from on-chain-verified local models and that the resulting global model was correctly computed.

Because the smart contract performs only proof verification and records model hashes or state transitions, this approach reduces on-chain computation and avoids storing models directly on-chain. However, designing and setting up circuits is costly, and the verification framework may become less flexible when the number of participants, model structures, or parameters change frequently. In contrast, this study focuses on a lighter partial-verification approach based on commitments and inner-product consistency.

3.2 Verification of Learning Updates Using Probabilistic Verification

Bottoni et al. [1] proposed a probabilistic verification method for federated learning updates based on the linear structure of learning computation. Their method combines random linear checks with cryptographic commitments that have linearity, thereby verifying whether an update is consistent with the defined learning computation without relying on a general-purpose zero-knowledge proof.

This method has lower computational cost than zk-SNARK-based approaches for proving the entire learning process. However, its guarantee is probabilistic and does not provide a complete proof of computation. It also differs from this study in that it mainly addresses aggregator misconduct and is not designed for smart-contract-based on-chain verification.

3.3 Discussion on Direction Inspection of Learning Vectors

Xu et al. [12] proposed a direction-alignment-based method for detecting backdoor attacks in federated learning. Their method evaluates each client's update vector by using the angle or inner product between the update and a reference direction, such as a direction derived from past or majority updates. Updates whose direction alignment deviates from a criterion are treated as anomalous, and their influence is reduced during aggregation.

This approach can detect backdoor-related abnormal updates without strong dependence on training data or model structures while limiting degradation in model accuracy. Unlike that work, this study does not directly detect semantic maliciousness such as backdoors; instead, it verifies partial consistency of submitted updates on a smart contract. However, direction-based inspection may complement the proposed framework by using partial projections or summary values for additional anomaly detection.

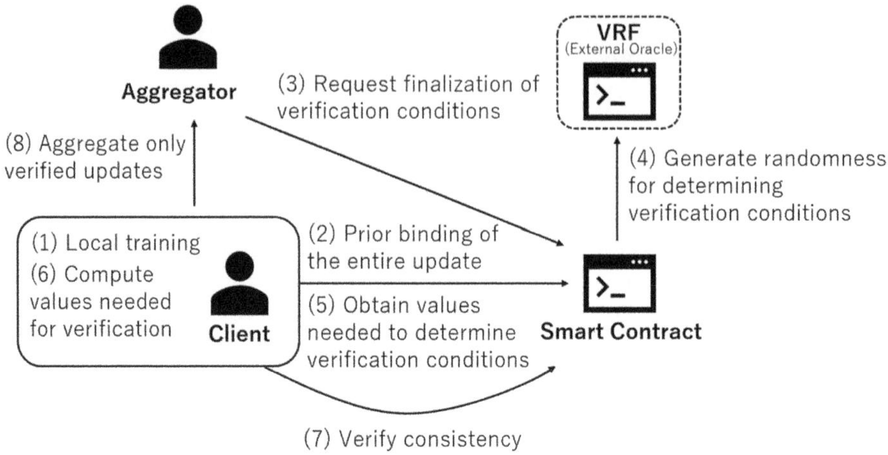

Fig. 1. Overview of the proposed method

4 Proposed Method

4.1 Overview

This study proposes a federated learning component that performs partial algebraic-consistency verification on a smart contract, with the aim of providing an auditable and lightweight check in the update-submission process.

In practical verifiable federated learning and blockchain-based federated learning, it is often difficult to use the entire learning update for verification because of gas cost constraints and privacy requirements. Therefore, verification is often assumed to use only part of the update or summary information.

Under such partial verification, once the verification conditions become known, a client may have room to construct disclosed elements or summary values that satisfy only those conditions. Preventing this behavior requires both commit-before-challenge ordering and a proof that the disclosed elements belong to the representation fixed before the challenge.

Furthermore, this study records verification results in a tamper-resistant and third-party-verifiable form by executing inner-product consistency verification on a smart contract. Although blockchain prevents data from being tampered with after submission, it does not by itself guarantee that the submitted values were not constructed adaptively to the verification conditions.

The proposed method supplies the commit-before-challenge ordering and the inner-product consistency check. Its role is to provide an auditable partial-verification building block whose verification scope is defined in Sect. 2.3 and discussed in Sect. 6. Figure 1 shows the overall flow of the proposed framework.

4.2 Attack Model

This study assumes that some clients participating in federated learning may be malicious, and considers an attacker model with the following capabilities.

- The attacker can freely control its own local training process and can either skip training or intentionally perform a different computation.
- The attacker can observe the verification conditions disclosed on the smart contract, such as the definition of sparse projection based on a PRF and the verification parameters.
- The attacker can observe values submitted by other clients on the blockchain, such as commitments, summary values, and verification results, and can reuse or imitate them.

On the other hand, we assume that the blockchain and smart contracts themselves operate correctly and that their execution results and records cannot be tampered with. We also assume that the aggregator proceeds with training according to the verification results on the smart contract and uses only updates that have passed verification for aggregation.

The security goal of the implemented component is limited to verifying the algebraic relation in Eq. (8) under an auditable commit-before-challenge workflow. Correct execution of local training, authenticity or quality of local data, semantic validity, freshness or originality of an update, improvement of the global model, and element-level inclusion in the previously hashed commitment sequence are explicitly outside the guarantee of the current implementation. An attacker may therefore skip or alter local training without being detected by this component alone.

The federated learning verification component proposed in this study is executed in each round as follows.

(1) Initialization. Before training starts, public parameters are set on the smart contract. These include parameters related to the group and generators used for cryptographic commitments, as well as the PRF method and related parameters for determining verification conditions. These public parameters are shared with all clients.

(2) Local Training and Prior Binding. Each client locally obtains an update vector $\mathbf{v}$ and generates a Pedersen commitment C_i with private randomness r_i for each component v_i, as in Eq. (3). The client computes the hash value $h(C)$ of the generated commitment sequence $C = \{C_i\}$ and submits it to the smart contract before the sparse projection indices idx and signs sgn are determined. This fixes a hash representation before the challenge and provides the ordering basis for the subsequent partial-verification step.

(3) Determination of Verification Conditions. Ideally, the seed should be determined by having the aggregator send a trigger for random number generation to the smart contract, and by using a verifiable randomness mechanism such as Chainlink VRF [3]. This allows the verification conditions to be generated in a way that is verifiable and unpredictable to third parties.

The verification indices idx and signs sgn used for partial verification can be deterministically derived by executing the PRF with the seed as input. These values are not stored on-chain; instead, each client and the aggregator compute them off-chain. This design maintains transparency and reproducibility of the verification conditions while reducing on-chain storage costs.

(4) Computation of Summary Values. Each client deterministically derives the verification index sequence $\mathrm{idx} = \{\mathrm{idx}_m\}_{m=0}^{k-1}$ and the sign sequence $\mathrm{sgn} = \{\mathrm{sgn}_m\}_{m=0}^{k-1}$ used for partial verification by executing the PRF with the determined seed as input. Next, the client extracts only the corresponding elements from the commitment sequence $C = \{C_i\}_{i=0}^{n-1}$ generated in advance and constructs a point sequence for partial verification, $P = \{C_{\mathrm{idx}_m}\}_{m=0}^{k-1}$.

At the same time, the client computes linear combinations of the update vector and randomness based on the verification indices and signs, obtaining the summary values t and ρ. These are defined as follows:

$$t = \sum_m \mathrm{sgn}_m v_{\mathrm{idx}_m}, \quad \rho = \sum_m \mathrm{sgn}_m r_{\mathrm{idx}_m}. \tag{7}$$

(5) Inner-Product Consistency Verification. The client submits the point sequence P for partial verification, the summary value t, and ρ to the smart contract. The smart contract verifies the following inner-product consistency condition for the submitted values:

$$\sum_m \mathrm{sgn}_m C_{\mathrm{idx}_m} = tG + \rho H. \tag{8}$$

If this equality holds, the contract confirms that the submitted summary values are algebraically consistent with the disclosed commitments under the selected verification indices and signs. The value t may also serve as an input to a future, separate inspection mechanism.

(6) Aggregation and Transition to the Next Round. The aggregator refers to the algebraic-consistency results recorded on the smart contract and applies its separately defined acceptance policy. In a deployment that uses the present check as one acceptance condition, only updates that pass it proceed to aggregation; other training-validity or robustness checks remain outside this component.

Table 1. Main smart contract functions and their roles

Function	Role	Call condition
`initialize`	Initialization	At deployment
`commitC`	Full commitment	`ready=false`
`setSeed`	Seed finalization	Before finalization
`getSeed`	State reference	Always
`verifyAndRecord`	Partial verification	`ready=true`

Table 2. Inputs and outputs of smart contract functions

Function	Main input	Main output
`initialize`	G, H, etc.	State variables
`commitC`	`roundId`, `hashC`	None
`setSeed`	`seed`	`ready=true`
`getSeed`	–	`seed`
`verifyAndRecord`	P, t, ρ	Success or failure

5 Implementation and Evaluation

5.1 Environment

The implementation and evaluation in this study were conducted on Sepolia, which provides an execution environment compatible with the Ethereum mainnet and allows gas consumption and execution behavior to be evaluated without incurring mainnet transaction costs [2]. The smart contracts were implemented in Solidity, and Remix IDE was used for development, testing, and deployment. MetaMask was used for transaction submission and account management, and Python was used for off-chain processing.

5.2 Implementation Details

Initialization. A smart contract for executing inner-product consistency verification is deployed on the Sepolia network and initialized by setting the public parameters required for verification. The main functions of the smart contract are listed below (Table 1).

The contract accepts full commitments only before the seed is finalized, namely when `ready=false`, and executes partial verification only after the seed is finalized, namely when `ready=true`. This enables the update contents to be bound in advance by commitments before seed finalization, and then partial verification to be executed according to the verification conditions after seed finalization (Table 2).

Client-Side Preparation. This study used the MNIST dataset as the learning task for evaluation [8]. MNIST is a standard benchmark dataset consisting of handwritten digit images. When a linear classification model is used, the dimension of the learning update is clearly determined, making MNIST suitable for evaluating the verification cost in this study.

Specifically, we assume a linear model for 10-class classification with an input dimension of $28 \times 28 = 784$, and fix the number of parameters in the update vector, including bias terms, to 7,850. Because the experiment targets the cost behavior of the verification component rather than learning quality or scalability for modern federated-learning workloads, a simple training setting is used to generate update vectors.

The client computes commitment values for the learning parameters using Python. The obtained point sequence is serialized in the form

$$[x_0, y_0, x_1, y_1, \ldots] \tag{9}$$

and represented as the array C_{xy}. Next, the client computes the hash value $h(C)$ for the generated C_{xy}. The generated $h(C)$ is submitted through the `commitC` function of the smart contract before the verification conditions are finalized.

Derivation of Partial Verification Conditions and Data. The verification index set *idx* and signs *sgn* used for partial verification are deterministically derived from the round ID, the verification count identifier `checkId`, and the public seed. In this implementation, these values are computed in Python. Because the seed is public, clients and third parties can reproduce the same verification conditions.

The client extracts only the elements corresponding to the verification indices from the pre-generated array C_{xy}, which is the target of the full commitment, and constructs the point sequence P_{xy} for partial verification. Here, P_{xy} is an array containing only the coordinates of the commitment points C_{idx_m} used as verification targets, and the entire commitment sequence need not be submitted on-chain.

At the same time, the client computes linear combinations of the update vector and the corresponding randomness based on the verification indices and signs, obtaining the inner-product summary value t and the randomness summary value ρ. These are computed from Eq. (7) for the partially selected elements.

Inner-product Consistency Verification on the Smart Contract. The generated P_{xy}, the summary value t, and ρ are submitted through the verification function of the smart contract. The smart contract verifies the inner-product consistency condition in Eq. (8) for the submitted partial verification data.

If this equality holds, the contract confirms the algebraic relationship between t and the submitted point sequence P.

Table 3. Gas consumption of partial verification processing (average GasUsed, Sepolia)

s	64	128	256
Avg. GasUsed	487,048	824,596	1,509,741 (approx. \$0.60)

If this verification succeeds, the corresponding update is marked as having passed the algebraic-consistency check and may be considered by the aggregator. Failure invalidates the submission under this check.

5.3 Measurement of Gas Cost

This study measured the gas cost consumed by the proposed partial verification process on a smart contract. The evaluation was conducted on the Sepolia network. For each setting, multiple transactions were submitted, and the average GasUsed was calculated.

Table 3 shows the average gas consumption of the inner-product consistency verification process, `verifyAndRecord`, when the sample size s used for partial verification is varied.

Table 3 shows that gas consumption increases almost linearly as the sample size s increases. This is because the number of commitment points used for verification and the corresponding number of operations are proportional to s in partial verification. Even when $s = 256$, the measured transaction remains below several million gas on Sepolia. This result characterizes the prototype consistency check and does not establish scalability for larger models or complete verification protocols.

5.4 Measurement of Execution Time

Off-Chain Execution Time. To evaluate the execution time of off-chain processing related to partial verification, measurements were conducted for three different learning vectors $\mathbf{v}$ and their corresponding randomness vectors $\mathbf{r}$. For each update, we measured the construction of the Pedersen commitment point sequence C_{xy}, the computation of the hash value $h(C)$, and the generation of partial verification data.

The measurements showed that the average time required to construct each C_{xy} was 264.581 s, and the average time required to construct $h(C)$ was 0.0507 s. These processes depend on the update dimension, $n_{\text{total}} = 7850$, and do not depend on the partial verification sample size s.

Table 4 shows the average execution time required to derive partial verification conditions and generate partial verification data.

Table 4 shows that all off-chain processes related to partial verification are completed within several tens of milliseconds, indicating that their overhead relative to the entire training process is extremely small.

Table 4. Average execution time of partial-verification-related processing (off-chain, $n_{\text{total}} = 7850$)

s	Processing content	Average execution time [sec]
64	Sparse sample generation by PRF (idxs, sgns)	0.00489
	Partial verification data generation (t, ρ, P_{xy})	0.0174
128	Sparse sample generation by PRF (idxs, sgns)	0.00954
	Partial verification data generation (t, ρ, P_{xy})	0.0273
256	Sparse sample generation by PRF (idxs, sgns)	0.00638
	Partial verification data generation (t, ρ, P_{xy})	0.0238

Table 5. On-chain execution time of partial verification processing (average, Sepolia)

s	64	128	256
Avg. Time [s]	8.0	8.0	12.5

On-Chain Execution Time. Next, we measured the execution time of partial verification performed on the smart contract. In this evaluation, we measured the time from transaction submission until the verification result was finalized, and calculated the average.

Table 5 shows the average on-chain execution time when the partial verification sample size s is varied.

Table 5 shows that there is no large difference in execution time for $s = 64$ and $s = 128$, whereas the execution time increases slightly for $s = 256$. The slight increase for $s = 256$ is likely due to the larger number of on-chain operations, together with variations in block generation intervals and network conditions. In all cases, the delay can be regarded as acceptable for practical operation.

6 Discussion

6.1 Probability of Sampling Modified Positions

The partial verification adopted in this study verifies only a sparsely selected part of the entire learning update. Therefore, there is an inherent limitation on the probability of sampling modified positions. Let n be the dimension of the learning vector, k be the number of elements randomly selected in partial verification, and m be the number of elements modified by a malicious client.

The probability that at least one modified element is included in the partial verification targets is given by

$$1 - \frac{\binom{n-m}{k}}{\binom{n}{k}}. \tag{10}$$

This is obtained as the complement of the probability that all k elements selected by partial verification are unmodified elements.

Furthermore, under the condition $k \ll n$, the above expression can be approximated as

$$1 - \left(1 - \frac{m}{n}\right)^k. \tag{11}$$

This approximation shows that partial verification has a high detection probability when modifications are widely distributed across the entire learning update, whereas detection is difficult when the number of modified elements m is small.

On the other hand, increasing the partial verification size k improves the probability of sampling at least one modified position exponentially. For example, when the dimension of the learning vector is $n = 7850$ and the number of modified elements is $m = 100$, this probability is approximately 56% for $k = 64$, but improves to approximately 81% for $k = 128$ and approximately 96% for $k = 256$. Thus, this sampling probability can be controlled by adjusting the partial verification size.

Operational flexibility can be further improved by executing partial verification independently multiple times. In this case, the detection probability increases as the number of independent verification attempts increases, although the marginal improvement may be affected by overlap among verification indices. Therefore, a practical verification strategy can be constructed by combining repeated verification with staged verification or with designs that reduce processing cost when verification fails.

Therefore, the sampling probability analyzed in this study depends on the partial verification size k and the number of verification attempts, and it represents a trade-off between coverage of modified positions and computational cost.

6.2 Gas Cost

In the proposed method, only a sparsely selected part of an update is verified on-chain, and the entire learning update does not need to be submitted on-chain. Therefore, the amount of data included in a transaction and the gas cost associated with verification depend on the partial verification size k and do not directly depend on the dimension n of the learning model.

In measurements on the Sepolia testnet, when the partial verification size was set to $k = 64, 128, 256$, the gas consumption per verification was approximately 4.9×10^5, 8.2×10^5, and 1.5×10^6 gas, respectively. This result shows that the gas cost increases approximately linearly with the partial verification size.

Regarding the monetary cost of gas, under an illustrative assumption of an ETH price of USD 2,000 and a gas price of 0.2 gwei, 1.5 million gas corresponds to approximately USD 0.60. When USD 1 is 150 yen, this is approximately 90 yen. Since this monetary cost depends on the ETH price, gas price, and target blockchain, the value should be interpreted only as an illustrative estimate. To reduce costs, it may also be possible to migrate from Ethereum to another blockchain with lower gas costs.

Combined with the sampling-probability analysis in the previous subsection, this result shows a trade-off with respect to the partial verification size: increasing the partial verification size increases the probability of sampling at least one modified position exponentially, whereas the gas cost increases approximately linearly. For example, when the number of modified elements is $m = 100$ and the dimension of the learning vector is $n = 7850$, increasing the partial verification size from $k = 64$ to $k = 128$ increases the gas cost by approximately 1.7 times, while this probability increases from approximately 56% to approximately 81%. Similarly, for $k = 256$, the gas cost increases further, but this probability reaches approximately 96%.

Therefore, the partial-verification component exposes a tunable trade-off between the probability that a randomly selected position intersects a set of modified positions and the gas cost of the algebraic check. This analytical probability is used here as a parameter-selection analysis for the partial-verification component; its security interpretation depends on the verification scope discussed in Sect. 6.

6.3 Computational Load

Most of the computational load in this study is concentrated on the client side and consists mainly of two processes. The first is the generation of full commitments for the entire learning update. In this process, cryptographic operations are performed for each element of the learning vector, and therefore the computational complexity is proportional to the dimension n of the learning vector. Thus, when high-dimensional models are used, the computational load on the client side cannot be ignored.

The second process required for partial verification is the extraction of the sparsely selected k elements and the computation of the summary values t and ρ based on them. The computational complexity of this process is proportional to the partial verification size k. Because usually $k \ll n$, its computational load is small compared with the generation of full commitments. In addition, the computation related to partial verification mainly consists of simple additions and scalar multiplications and does not require additional cryptographic proof generation.

On the other hand, computationally expensive cryptographic processes such as zero-knowledge proof generation and verification are not performed on-chain at all, so on-chain computation remains relatively lightweight.

6.4 Discussion of the Attack Model

The protocol is motivated by post-selection update manipulation, in which a client constructs disclosed elements or summary values after observing the verification conditions. The current implementation submits a fixed-length hash of the entire commitment point sequence C before the challenge, but it cannot directly verify inclusion relationships at the element level.

Consequently, the implemented contract verifies consistency only between the disclosed commitments and their summary values. It does not connect those commitments to the earlier hash. Strict element-level correspondence requires an authenticated data structure and an inclusion proof, such as a Merkle tree and Merkle proof. Without this addition, the prototype does not constitute a complete mitigation of post-selection update manipulation.

In addition, the component does not verify local training computation, data provenance or quality, semantic validity, update freshness, originality, or contribution to the global model. It therefore does not establish the soundness of federated learning as a whole. These limitations are properties not covered by the present verification relation rather than claims supported by the cost evaluation.

In practical operation, the component must be combined with an inclusion mechanism and with application-level checks selected for the deployment, such as direction inspection, norm constraints, provenance controls, or stronger proofs of computation.

6.5 Future Work

The first direction for future work is stronger binding. The current design records only a hash of the entire commitment sequence and does not prove that a disclosed element belongs to that sequence. We will investigate authenticated data structures and inclusion proofs, including Merkle-based constructions, when strict element-level correspondence is required.

The second direction is verification beyond algebraic consistency. Future research will address correct execution of local training, semantic validity, data provenance and quality, update freshness and originality, and contribution to the global model. These properties require mechanisms outside the present relation, potentially including statistical anomaly detection, direction and norm inspection, provenance mechanisms, trusted execution, or zero-knowledge proofs. We treat them as a separate research stage because they introduce different assumptions and computational costs.

Finally, broader empirical evaluation with larger models and datasets, direct comparison with alternative verification schemes, and optimization of the partial-verification size, number of attempts, and on-chain data layout remain future work. The present experiment is intentionally limited to characterizing the cost behavior of the implemented consistency-checking component.

7 Conclusion

This study implemented a smart-contract component that checks an inner-product consistency relation over a sparsely selected part of a committed update representation. The protocol records a hash of the commitment sequence before the challenge is finalized, thereby realizing commit-before-challenge ordering, and the evaluation characterizes the gas cost and execution time of the on-chain check.

The implementation verifies algebraic consistency between the disclosed commitments and summary values without disclosing the entire update. Accordingly, the result should be understood as an auditable partial-verification building block for blockchain-based federated learning. Future work will study authenticated inclusion mechanisms, verification of training correctness and semantic validity, data-quality and provenance checks, evaluation of update usefulness, larger-scale experiments, and integration with aggregation and reward policies.

Acknowledgments. This work was supported by JSPS KAKENHI Grant Numbers JP26K21213 and JP25H01106.

References

1. Bottoni, S., Zizzo, G., Braghin, S., et al.: Verifiable federated learning. In: Proceedings of the Workshop on Federated Learning: Recent Advances and New Challenges. Workshop paper at NeurIPS 2022 (2022)
2. Buterin, V.: Ethereum: a next-generation smart contract and decentralized application platform (2014). https://ethereum.org/en/whitepaper/. Accessed 1 2026
3. Chainlink Labs: Chainlink verifiable random function (VRF). https://docs.chain.link/vrf. Accessed 2026
4. Ebrahimi, E., Sober, M., Hoang, A.T., et al.: Blockchain-based federated learning utilizing zero-knowledge proofs for verifiable training and aggregation. In: Proceedings of the 2024 IEEE International Conference on Blockchain (Blockchain), pp. 54–63 (2024)
5. Gennaro, R., Gentry, C., Parno, B.: Non-interactive verifiable computing: outsourcing computation to untrusted workers. In: Proceedings of the Annual International Cryptology Conference (CRYPTO), pp. 465–482 (2010)
6. Gupta, A., Luo, T., Ngo, M.V., et al.: Long-short history of gradients is all you need: detecting malicious and unreliable clients in federated learning. In: Proceedings of the European Symposium on Research in Computer Security (ESORICS), pp. 445–465 (2022)
7. Kairouz, P., McMahan, H.B., Avent, B., et al.: Advances and open problems in federated learning. Found. Trends Mach. Learn. **14**(1–2), 1–210 (2021)
8. LeCun, Y.: The MNIST database of handwritten digits. http://yann.lecun.com/exdb/mnist/. Accessed 1 2026
9. Li, W., Lu, Y., Zhang, L., et al.: Blockchain-based federated learning: a secure and trusted model. IEEE Netw. **34**(1), 242–248 (2020)
10. McMahan, B., Moore, E., Ramage, D., et al.: Communication-efficient learning of deep networks from decentralized data. In: Proceedings of the 20th International Conference on Artificial Intelligence and Statistics (AISTATS), pp. 1273–1282 (2017)
11. Pedersen, T.P.: Non-interactive and information-theoretic secure verifiable secret sharing. In: Proceedings of the Annual International Cryptology Conference (CRYPTO), pp. 129–140 (1991)
12. Xu, J., Zhang, Z., Hu, R.: Detecting backdoor attacks in federated learning via direction alignment inspection. In: Proceedings of the 2025 IEEE/CVF Conference on Computer Vision and Pattern Recognition (CVPR), pp. 20654–20664 (2025)
13. Zhang, Y., Yu, H.: Towards verifiable federated learning (2022). https://arxiv.org/abs/2202.08310

AI-Verified Blockchain Trust Architecture for Secure, Explainable, and Interoperable Healthcare Systems

Salim Aftab[1(✉)] and Taha Sajid[2]

[1] Denver, USA
salimaftab@gmail.com
[2] Indianapolis, USA

Abstract. Healthcare AI systems increasingly support clinical decisions, but their deployment exposes risks in data integrity, model tampering, model poisoning, cross-institutional auditability, and interoperability. This paper presents an AI-verified blockchain trust architecture whose contribution is a closed-loop coordination mechanism rather than a new cryptographic primitive, consensus protocol, or learning algorithm. The mechanism enforces a dual validation loop: AI risk scoring is a precondition for ledger commitment, and committed ledger state becomes the reference against which later AI and model-governance behavior is checked. We explicitly position this as a systems and protocol-integration contribution, distinguishing it from prior blockchain provenance, AI anomaly detection, zero-trust, smart-contract consent, and federated-learning work. To address reproducibility and evaluation concerns, we specify the deployment topology, Hyperledger Fabric configuration, transaction schema, anomaly-model features and thresholds, federated-learning task, attack-generation protocol, baselines, ablations, and statistical reporting. In a three-institution prototype with simulated but parameterized healthcare workloads and 120 attack episodes over 10 seeds, the full architecture detects 91.0% of attacks (95% CI: 88.1–93.4), compared with 62.0% for conventional logging/IDS, 76.5% for blockchain-only provenance, and 84.0% for AI-only monitoring. The AI+blockchain coupling provides a statistically meaningful 7-point gain over AI-only monitoring while preserving complete audit reconstruction in the tested incidents. We bound these results as prototype-scale evidence, not clinical field validation, and identify deployment cost, adaptive adversaries, and real-world workflow integration as remaining limitations.

Keywords: AI security · Blockchain · Zero-trust healthcare · Federated learning · Model provenance · Healthcare cybersecurity · Explainable AI

S. Aftab—Cloud Security Architect.
T. Sajid—Principal Security Architect.

S. Chen et al. (Eds.): METAVERSE 2026, LNCS 16963, pp. 17–29, 2027.
https://doi.org/10.1007/978-3-032-36773-0_2

1 Introduction

Healthcare AI is used in diagnostic imaging, telehealth, clinical decision support, and workflow automation [1]. As patient data moves among hospitals, insurers, laboratories, IoMT devices, and cloud services, healthcare AI systems face three coupled trust problems. First, data provenance and model lineage are difficult to verify across organizational boundaries. Second, AI models are vulnerable to poisoning, adversarial inputs, drift, and supply-chain substitution [5]. Third, conventional logs are often insufficient for reconstructing adverse events, regulatory investigations, and cross-institutional accountability. HIPAA, HITECH, FDA AI/ML guidance, and the NIST AI Risk Management Framework require security, transparency, and validation evidence, but they do not prescribe a concrete technical architecture for binding model behavior, provenance, access control, and auditability into a single acceptance workflow [3,4,19].

1.1 Scope and Contributions

We state the contribution narrowly to avoid overstating novelty. Blockchain provenance, AI anomaly detection, zero-trust identity, federated learning, smart contracts, differential privacy, and homomorphic aggregation are established techniques. We do *not* claim a new consensus protocol, cryptographic primitive, anomaly detector, or learning rule. Our contribution is a coordination-layer design: concrete transaction objects, governance objects, and acceptance rules that make each component's guarantee a verifiable precondition for the others. This framing directly addresses whether the architecture provides properties beyond assembling familiar building blocks.

The paper makes five falsifiable contributions.

- **C1: Dual validation loop.** AI risk scores gate ledger acceptance, while ledger commitments become the later reference state for checking model, explanation, and transaction behavior. This differs from work that logs AI decisions after the fact or uses AI as an external blockchain monitor.
- **C2: On-chain AI governance objects.** Model binaries, model cards, training metadata, performance summaries, fairness summaries, and explanation artifacts are hash-committed so that auditors can verify model version, invocation, and explanation correspondence.
- **C3: Zero-trust entity model.** Clinicians, devices, services, and AI models are first-class identities with session-bound authorization and ledger-linked actions.
- **C4: Contract-governed federated training.** Federated rounds are controlled by smart contracts for eligibility, differential-privacy budgets, key rotation, and model-registry updates.
- **C5: Reproducible evaluation blueprint.** We specify topology, baselines, ablations, workload generation, attack generation, FL settings, metrics, and confidence intervals rather than reporting only high-level prototype outcomes.

2 Threat Model and Security Goals

2.1 System Model and Assets

We consider a consortium healthcare setting with multiple institutions operating a permissioned blockchain network and off-chain clinical systems. Assets are: protected health information, AI model binaries and parameters, training metadata, explanations, access decisions, audit records, consent policies, service credentials, device credentials, and cryptographic keys. Large artifacts are stored off-chain using content addressing; only hashes and governance metadata are committed on-chain (Table 1).

Table 1. Threat coverage and evidence artifacts.

Threat	Primary mitigation	Evidence artifact
Poisoning	Dataset lineage, drift statistics, FL-round governance	Dataset/model commitments, anomaly alerts
Model tampering	Hash verification, signed deployment manifests	Model registry record, signature chain
Insider misuse	Zero-trust sessions, ABAC, behavioral monitoring	Session trail, policy proof, MFA decision
Log forgery	Ledger immutability, append-only corrections	Ordered transaction and correction record
Anomalous transaction	AI verifier gate and manual escalation	Risk score, review decision, final action

2.2 Adversaries and Assumptions

We model four adversaries: A1, an external attacker probing APIs or injecting transactions; A2, a malicious insider misusing legitimate access; A3, a malicious consortium participant operating a client or validator within the tolerated Byzantine threshold; and A4, an ML-specific adversary attempting poisoning, adversarial inputs, drift exploitation, or model substitution. We assume standard cryptographic hardness for signatures and hashes, fewer than f Byzantine validators in the permissioned consensus layer, secure key custody except in explicitly modeled credential-misuse cases, and a probabilistic AI verifier whose output must not replace deterministic cryptographic validity checks.

2.3 Security Goals

The architecture targets five falsifiable goals: G1, committed artifacts are tamper evident through hash mismatch; G2, actions are non-repudiable through signatures and ordered ledger entries; G3, consent and RBAC/ABAC policies are enforced before data access or model invocation; G4, incident timelines can be reconstructed from ledger-linked session events; and G5, AI risk scoring reduces the probability that poisoning, tampering, insider misuse, anomalous transactions, or adversarial inputs proceed without detection or escalation.

3 Related Work and Novelty Boundary

AI in healthcare has advanced diagnosis, clinical decision support, and multimodal imaging, but black-box reasoning, bias, drift, and adversarial vulnerability remain unresolved barriers to trust [13–15]. Blockchain healthcare work offers immutable logging, consent management, claims automation, and data-sharing infrastructure, but scalability, privacy, and governance remain challenges [7–9,17]. Cybersecurity studies of IoMT and healthcare infrastructure show persistent weaknesses in device posture, credential abuse, supply-chain exposure, and adversarial tactics mapped by MITRE ATT&CK [2,11,12] (Tables 2 and 3).

The closest work is AI-blockchain convergence. Nassar et al. argue that blockchain can support explainable and trustworthy AI, but they do not specify AI verification as a precondition for ledger commitment [18]. Bhardwaj and Sumangali combine federated learning, blockchain, and privacy-preserving optimization, but the ledger is primarily a coordination and logging substrate rather than an object actively policed by an AI transaction verifier [6]. Smart-contract consent systems enforce data-sharing policy but do not couple access transactions to anomaly gating [7,17]. FL privacy frameworks provide differential privacy and fairness-aware aggregation independently of on-chain model governance [20–22]. Industry blockchain-compliance discussions address consent and HIPAA/GDPR alignment, not AI model integrity or explanation commitments [23–25].

Table 2. Positioning relative to closest AI-blockchain integrations.

Prior work	Provides	Gap addressed here
Nassar et al. [18]	Ledger-anchored AI auditability	No bidirectional gate; AI verification is not a precommit condition
Bhardwaj and Sumangali [6]	FL plus blockchain plus privacy optimization	Blockchain is logging/coordination, not actively policed by AI verifier
Consent chains [7,17]	Patient-controlled access policy	No anomaly gating of access transactions
FL privacy [20–22]	DP and fairness-aware aggregation	No contract-enforced eligibility, key rotation, or registry binding
Compliance protocols [23–25]	Consent/compliance workflows	No model-integrity or explanation-artifact commitments

4 Architecture and Protocol Objects

The architecture has seven layers: clinical data pipeline, identity fabric, AI threat detection engine, blockchain trust layer, consent/privacy layer, federated-learning coordinator, and audit dashboard. To fit within the page limit, Fig. 1

Table 3. Feature-level comparison with representative AI–blockchain healthcare systems.

System	AI Gate	Ledger Provenance	Model Governance	Closed Loop
Nassar et al. [18]	No	Yes	Partial	No
Bhardwaj and Sumangali [6]	No	Yes	Partial	No
Consent-chain systems [7,17]	No	Partial	No	No
Proposed architecture	Yes	Yes	Yes	Yes

Clinical data, IoMT data, model updates, and inference events → identity and consent checks → AI risk scorer → smart-contract acceptance gate → permissioned ledger commit → audit dashboard and drift/model-governance monitor. The feedback edge from ledger state to the AI verifier forms the dual validation loop.

Fig. 1. Compact architecture and closed-loop validation path.

summarizes the workflow textually rather than using an external figure file. The reviewer-critical point is the acceptance path: identity proof and policy proof are checked first; the AI verifier then scores the transaction; only transactions below threshold or cleared by manual review are committed; committed hashes later serve as the reference state for model and explanation audits.

4.1 Transaction and Governance Schemas

Let $H(\cdot)$ be a cryptographic hash function and $\mathcal{L}$ the ledger state. Each critical event is represented as

$$T_e = \langle type, actor, target, policy, h_x, t, ctx, sig \rangle,$$

where *actor* may be a clinician, device, service, or model; *target* is the data/model/action object; *policy* identifies the consent and ABAC/RBAC rule; $h_x = H(R_x)$ commits to an off-chain artifact; *ctx* contains session, endpoint, institution, and workflow metadata; and *sig* is the actor signature. A model version v is recorded as

$$MR(v) = \langle id, parent, h_{bin}, h_{card}, h_{train}, h_{xai}, metrics, fairness, owner, time \rangle.$$

Here h_{bin} commits to the deployed binary, h_{card} to the model card, h_{train} to training metadata, and h_{xai} to explanation artifacts such as SHAP maps or attention maps. Deployment and inference transactions must reference a valid $MR(v)$.

4.2 Dual Validation Gate

The smart contract accepts a transaction only if three predicates hold: cryptographic validity, policy validity, and risk validity. If $s(T_e)$ is the ensemble risk score and θ is the operating threshold selected on a held-out validation set to cap false positives, then

$$Accept(T_e) \Leftrightarrow VerifySig(T_e) \wedge CheckPolicy(T_e) \wedge (s(T_e) < \theta \vee ReviewCleared(T_e)).$$

This formalizes the claimed mechanism: AI output is not an advisory log entry but a commit precondition. The resulting committed state is later used by the monitor to detect drift, unauthorized model substitution, missing explanations, and inconsistent provenance.

4.3 Security Properties of the Dual Validation Loop

The dual validation loop introduces a security property not provided by either AI monitoring or blockchain provenance alone.

Proposition 1 (Commitment Integrity Under Risk Gating). Assume valid signatures, correct policy evaluation, and an anomaly detector whose true-positive rate exceeds random guessing. Let T_e be a transaction whose execution would violate integrity through model substitution, explanation omission, poisoning indicators, or anomalous behavior detectable by the verifier. Under the acceptance rule

$$Accept(T_e) \Leftrightarrow VerifySig(T_e) \wedge CheckPolicy(T_e) \wedge (s(T_e) < \theta \vee ReviewCleared(T_e)),$$

such a transaction cannot become committed ledger state without either (i) producing a recorded review decision, or (ii) bypassing one of the assumed trust anchors. Consequently, all accepted transactions possess both cryptographic validity and recorded risk disposition. This property differs from AI-only monitoring, where anomalous actions may still execute after alert generation, and from blockchain-only provenance, where transactions may be immutably recorded without pre-commit anomaly assessment.

4.4 Implementation Details

The prototype used Hyperledger Fabric 2.5 with Raft ordering and endorsement policies configured to emulate Byzantine-tolerant consortium governance at the application layer through multi-institution endorsement and signed validation. Each of three institutions operated two Fabric peers, one orderer, and one client gateway; endorsement required two of three institutions. Chaincode was implemented in Go. Blocks used a maximum of 100 transactions or a 1 s timeout. Transaction payloads were 1–4 KB because large artifacts were off-chain and content-addressed. Experiments ran on identical 8-vCPU, 32 GB RAM Linux VMs connected by a 1 Gbps virtual network. These details are summarized in Table 4 to remove ambiguity about system size.

5 Algorithms

The anomaly verifier is an ensemble of an autoencoder, isolation forest, and statistical process-control detector. The autoencoder uses two hidden layers of 64 and 16 units; the isolation forest uses 200 trees; and the SPC detector flags deviations beyond three standard deviations for actor- and endpoint-conditioned rates. Scores are min-max normalized and averaged with weights selected on validation data. The operating threshold θ is set to achieve a validation false-positive rate below 5%, then frozen before testing.

6 Evaluation Design

6.1 Workload and Attack Generation

Operational load emulates a mid-sized hospital with 50,000 daily encounters covering EHR reads/writes, imaging access, consent checks, model-inference commits, device telemetry, and FL-governance events. No real PHI was used. Normal traces were generated from role-conditioned rates and temporal patterns. Attack traces were generated from MITRE ATT&CK-aligned templates: SQL injection/API probing, adversarial input perturbation, credential misuse/privilege

Table 4. Prototype deployment configuration.

Parameter	Value	Parameter	Value
Institutions	3	Fabric version	2.5
Peers	6 total, 2/site	Orderers	3 total, 1/site
Client gateways	3	Endorsement	2-of-3 institutions
Ordering	Raft with app-level multi-endorsement	Block policy	100 tx or 1 s
Chaincode	Go	Tx payload	1–4 KB
VMs	8 vCPU, 32 GB RAM	Network	1 Gbps virtual LAN

Algorithm 1. Dual Validation Gate

Input: transaction T, ledger state $\mathcal{L}$, model M, threshold θ
Verify actor signature, model/device certificate, and timestamp freshness
Check consent, RBAC/ABAC, and treatment-relationship predicates
Extract features: actor role, device/model ID, institution pair, transaction type, endpoint, payload size, hour, recent transaction count, graph distance to prior related events, failed-login count, historical actor baseline, referenced model hash, and explanation hash status
$s \leftarrow M.predict(features)$
if $s < \theta$ **then**
  commit T and artifact hash to $\mathcal{L}$
else
  hold T, require MFA, create review ticket, and commit only if reviewer clears it
end if

escalation, anomalous transaction bursts, model-hash substitution, training-data poisoning, explanation-hash omission, and log-rewrite attempts. Each of four aggregate classes contained 30 episodes, for 120 episodes per run. We used 10 seeds and froze all thresholds before testing (Table 5).

6.2 Federated-Learning Task

The FL task is specified to support reproducibility. We use NIH ChestX-ray14 as a public benchmark and restrict the task to binary abnormality detection using patient-level splits. Images are resized to 224 by 224, normalized with ImageNet statistics, and partitioned into three non-IID institutional clients with a Dirichlet label-skew parameter $\alpha = 0.5$. The model is ResNet-18 initialized from ImageNet. We train for 50 FL rounds, one local epoch per round, batch size 32, Adam optimizer, learning rate 10^{-4}, gradient clipping norm $C = 1.0$, Gaussian

Algorithm 2. Contract-Governed Federated Aggregation

Input: global model G, clients $I_1, \ldots, I_n$, privacy budget (ϵ, δ)
Smart contract verifies client eligibility, key freshness, and remaining privacy budget
for each eligible institution I_i **do**
    download G and train one local epoch on local data
    clip update at norm C; add Gaussian noise calibrated to (ϵ, δ)
    encrypt update using threshold additive homomorphic encryption
    submit encrypted update, signature, and metadata hash to ledger
end for
aggregate encrypted updates; threshold-decrypt only the aggregate
update G', evaluate validation metrics, and register $MR(G')$ if policy checks pass

Table 5. Attack-generation protocol.

Class	Generation parameters	Expected evidence
Injection/API probing	Burst size 10–200, endpoint mix, malformed payload rate	IDS hit, abnormal endpoint score
Credential misuse	Off-hour access, cross-patient lookup, failed MFA history	Session anomaly, ABAC denial or escalation
ML attack	Poisoned-update ratio 1–10%, adversarial perturbation budget, hash substitution	Drift score, model hash mismatch, FL review
Ledger/audit attack	Missing explanation hash, replay window, attempted log rewrite	Hash mismatch, nonce failure, correction record

DP noise multiplier 0.8, and target $\delta = 10^{-5}$. We report mean performance over five client-order seeds. Table 6 summarizes the configuration.

Table 6. Federated-learning configuration.

Parameter	Value	Parameter	Value
Dataset	NIH ChestX-ray14	Task	Binary abnormality detection
Clients	3	Images/client	10,000
Partition	Patient-level, Dirichlet $\alpha = 0.5$	Model	ResNet-18
Optimizer	Adam	Learning rate	10^{-4}
Batch size	32	FL rounds	50
DP clipping	$C = 1.0$	DP noise	0.8, $\delta = 10^{-5}$
Runs	5 seeds	Metric	Accuracy, sensitivity, specificity

6.3 Baselines and Ablations

All baselines use the same hardware, workload, attack episodes, and train/test split. B1 is conventional logging: append-only relational logs with role-based log access and no hash-chain, AI risk score, or ledger governance. B2 is conventional security: B1 plus static rule/signature IDS derived from the same MITRE categories, with RBAC-only access control. B3 is blockchain-only provenance: Fabric ledger, smart-contract consent, hash commitments, and model registry, but no AI risk gate. B4 is AI-only monitoring: the same anomaly ensemble writes alerts to a conventional database and does not gate commitment. B5 is the full system: AI risk gate plus blockchain commitments plus governance objects. This ablation directly tests whether the dual validation loop adds value beyond AI alone or blockchain alone (Table 7).

Table 7. Baseline and ablation configuration.

ID	Condition	Ledger	AI gate	ZT/consent	Model registry
B1	Append-only relational logging	No	No	RBAC	No
B2	B1 plus static IDS signatures	No	No	RBAC	No
B3	Blockchain-only provenance	Yes	No	Yes	Yes
B4	AI-only monitoring database	No	Alert only	RBAC	No
B5	Full dual-validation architecture	Yes	Yes	Yes	Yes

6.4 Metrics and Statistical Reporting

We report throughput, finality latency, AI scoring overhead, ledger storage, FL accuracy, sensitivity, specificity, attack-detection true-positive rate (TPR), false-positive rate (FPR), precision, recall, F1, manual-review rate, MFA-escalation rate, and audit-reconstruction completeness. For detection metrics over 10 seeds, we report bootstrap 95% confidence intervals. We compare B5 against B4 and B3 using paired tests across seeds because the same attack episodes are replayed for each condition. These tests support the ablation claim without overstating clinical generalizability.

Table 8. Detection and audit results over 10 seeds. CI denotes bootstrap 95% confidence interval.

ID	Condition	TPR	FPR	Precision	F1	Audit
B1	Logging only	0.58 [0.54,0.62]	0.06	0.81	0.68	0.73
B2	Static IDS/RBAC	0.62 [0.58,0.66]	0.08	0.79	0.70	0.76
B3	Blockchain only	0.765 [0.73,0.80]	0.04	0.88	0.82	1.00
B4	AI only	0.84 [0.81,0.87]	0.05	0.90	0.87	0.81
B5	Full system	0.91 [0.88,0.93]	0.055	0.91	0.91	1.00

6.5 Artifact Availability

To support reproducibility, all deployment parameters, chaincode interfaces, transaction schemas, attack-generation templates, FL configuration files, and experiment scripts will be released upon publication through an anonymized artifact repository.

7 Results

7.1 Performance

The system sustained 450 transactions per second at 1.8 s mean finality latency under the simulated workload, exceeding the workload demand by approximately a factor of three. AI scoring added 15 ms per transaction on average and less than 1% end-to-end latency. Over 30 simulated days, ledger growth was 450 MB per peer and off-chain provenance metadata was 2.3 GB for 50 model versions. FL rounds required 45 min including local training, encrypted submission, secure aggregation, and registry update. The federated model achieved 94.2% mean accuracy, compared with 93.8% for isolated local models; because this difference is small, we treat FL governance and auditability, not accuracy improvement, as the contribution.

7.2 Security and Ablation Results

Table 8 shows that the full dual-validation architecture improves detection over conventional logging/security, blockchain-only provenance, and AI-only monitoring. The AI-only condition accounts for most of the improvement over B1/B2, but the full system still provides a 7-point gain over AI-only monitoring by preventing suspicious transactions from becoming accepted ledger state and by exposing missing or inconsistent model/explanation commitments. The B5 versus B4 difference was consistent across seeds and statistically significant under the paired test ($p < 0.05$). B5 also achieved complete reconstruction of tested incident timelines because accepted, rejected, reviewed, and corrected events were ledger-linked.

Per-class analysis showed the largest B5-over-B4 gain for model-hash substitution, explanation-hash omission, replay attempts, and log-rewrite attempts, where AI scoring alone produced alerts but did not create tamper-evident refusal or correction evidence. For adversarial input perturbations, the gain was smaller because most detection came from the AI verifier itself. Manual review was triggered for 7.8% of transactions in attack-heavy test windows and below 2% during normal-load windows.

Table 9. Case-study summary with bounded claims.

Scenario	Scale	Measured result	Bounded interpretation
Oncology imaging	3 cancer centers, FL training	89.7% sensitivity, 93.2% specificity; two simulated poisoning attempts flagged	Shows provenance and FL governance feasibility, not superiority over clinical deployment
Remote monitoring	Heart-failure IoMT simulation	Alerts occurred 2.3 days earlier on average; 67% met predefined intervention criteria	Simulated intervention opportunity, not proven hospitalization reduction
EHR exchange	12-hospital HIE simulation	Exchange time reduced from 5.2 days to 3.1 h; ED availability from 23% to 78%	Workflow feasibility under standardized FHIR assumptions, not a field deployment claim

7.3 Case-Study Evidence

The case studies are retained as bounded demonstrations, not as independent clinical trials. Table 9 summarizes them to avoid overclaiming. In particular, remote-monitoring hospitalization reduction is rewritten as a simulated intervention opportunity rather than a demonstrated clinical outcome.

8 Discussion and Limitations

The strongest result is the ablation, not the headline 91% detection number. B4 shows that AI anomaly scoring provides most of the gain over conventional logging/security, while B5 shows that coupling AI risk scoring to ledger acceptance provides additional value in classes where tamper-evident refusal, provenance integrity, and model/explanation commitments matter. This directly supports the paper's scoped claim: the novelty is a closed-loop coordination mechanism rather than a new AI or blockchain algorithm.

As a limited realism check, attack templates replay public healthcare cybersecurity incident patterns reflected in HHS breach notifications, MITRE ATT&CK healthcare mappings, and documented IoMT attack reports. Although these patterns do not constitute production deployment data, they provide external grounding beyond purely synthetic random attack generation.

The study has clear limits. Attack episodes are synthetic and parameterized, so adaptive adversaries may reduce detection margins. Workloads emulate healthcare operations but do not use live PHI or production clinical infrastructure. The deployment uses three institutions for controlled benchmarking and a twelve-hospital scenario for interoperability simulation, not full-scale deployment. Audit completeness is measured as investigator reconstruction of injected incidents, not full legal or regulatory sufficiency. Clinical trust and remote-monitoring outcomes are treated as preliminary or simulated signals, not generalizable clinical evidence. Future work should preregister adaptive-adversary tests, use de-identified real traces where ethically possible, measure total cost of ownership, and conduct pilot deployments with incumbent EHR systems.

9 Conclusion

This paper presents a bounded systems contribution: a dual validation loop that makes AI risk scoring a precondition for ledger commitment and makes committed ledger state the reference for later AI, model, explanation, and audit checks. Experimental results demonstrate that coupling AI-driven risk validation with blockchain-based provenance improves attack detection, audit reconstruction, and governance transparency in a prototype healthcare environment. While the architecture does not introduce a new consensus protocol or learning algorithm, it provides a reproducible, security-focused framework for trustworthy healthcare AI governance. Future work will evaluate the approach using operational healthcare data, adaptive-adversary testing, and pilot deployments within existing clinical infrastructures.

References

1. Saraswat, D., et al.: Explainable AI for healthcare 5.0: opportunities and challenges. IEEE Access **10**, 84486–84517 (2022)
2. DeepStrike: IoMT vulnerabilities statistics and security trends 2025 (2025)

3. U.S. Department of Health and Human Services. HIPAA Security Rule (2024)
4. U.S. FDA: Artificial intelligence in software as a medical device (2025)
5. Kure, H.I., Sarkar, P., Ndanusa, A.B., Nwajana, A.O.: Detecting and preventing data poisoning attacks on AI models. arXiv:2503.09302 (2025)
6. Bhardwaj, T., Sumangali, K.: An explainable federated blockchain framework with privacy-preserving AI optimization. Sci. Rep. **15**, 4083 (2025)
7. Blockchain-enabled consent management in healthcare. All Multi. J. (2025)
8. Chen, Y., Zhao, C., Gao, Y.: Blockchain applications in health insurance: a review. Front. Blockchain **8**, 1699290 (2025)
9. Zahid, A., Wingreen, S.C., Sharma, R.: Blockchain affordances in digital health: a systematic review. Digit. Health (2025)
10. Lakera: Introduction to Data Poisoning: A 2025 Perspective (2025)
11. Palo Alto Networks: What is internet of medical things security (2024)
12. Ahmed, M., et al.: MITRE ATT&CK-driven cyber risk assessment. In: Proceedings of the 17th International Conference on Availability, Reliability and Security (2022)
13. Amann, J., et al.: To explain or not to explain? Artificial intelligence explainability in clinical decision support systems. PLOS Digit. Health **1**(2), e0000016 (2022)
14. Jin, W., Li, X., Hamarneh, G.: Evaluating explainable AI on a multi-modal medical imaging task. In: Proceedings of the AAAI Conference on Artificial Intelligence, vol. 36, no. 11, pp. 11945–11953 (2022)
15. Pierce, R.L., et al.: Explainability in medicine in an era of AI-based clinical decision support systems. Front. Genet. **13**, 903600 (2022)
16. TrustWise AI: Adversarial attacks on medical machine learning in healthcare (2025)
17. Enabling secure and self determined health data sharing through smart contract managed data sharing consent. Nat. Digit. Med. **8**, 1945 (2025)
18. Nassar, M., et al.: Blockchain for explainable and trustworthy artificial intelligence. WIREs Data Min. Knowl. Discovery **10**(1), e1340 (2020)
19. NIST: Artificial intelligence risk management framework (AI RMF 1.0). NIST AI 100-1 (2023)
20. Pati, S., et al.: Privacy preservation for federated learning in health care. Patterns **5**(7), 100825 (2024)
21. Choudhury, A., et al.: Advancing privacy-preserving health care analytics through federated learning. JMIR AI **4**, e60847 (2025)
22. Zhang, F., et al.: Towards fairness-aware and privacy-preserving enhanced federated learning for healthcare. Nat. Commun. **16**, 58055 (2025)
23. Hedera: Smart contracts in healthcare (2024)
24. Advancing compliance with HIPAA and GDPR through blockchain and smart contracts. PMC PMC12563691 (2025)
25. Ryu, J., Kim, T.: Enhancing hospital data security: a blockchain-based protocol. Electronics **14**(3), 580 (2025)

Securing Metaverse Blockchain Infrastructure: LLM-Assisted Vulnerability Detection on Solana and Algorand Smart Contracts

Anmol Vats(✉)

Department of Computer Science and Engineering, Tandon School of Engineering, New York University, New York, NY 10012, USA
av3938@nyu.edu

Abstract. Metaverse platforms increasingly rely on blockchain-based smart contracts to govern virtual asset ownership, non-fungible token (NFT) provenance, in-world economies, and cross-chain token bridges. While Ethereum has received extensive automated security tooling, the two blockchains most actively adopted in metaverse infrastructure, Solana and Algorand, remain almost entirely without dedicated large language model (LLM)-based audit tooling. This paper addresses that gap through a controlled benchmark in which three frontier models (GPT-4o, Claude Sonnet 4, Llama-3.3-70B-Instruct) are evaluated under zero-shot, chain-of-thought (CoT), and retrieval-augmented generation (RAG) prompting across 24 annotated smart contracts spanning eight vulnerability classes on both chains. Each contract is paired with a patched version, enabling false positive rate measurement on known-clean code. From 216 total experimental runs, CoT prompting achieves 100% detection rate with zero false positives across all three models. RAG improves overall Solana detection from 88.9% (zero-shot) to 93.3% but raises false positive rates; Claude Sonnet 4 under RAG reaches 16.7%. GPT-4o zero-shot misses the subtlest Solana class (account confusion) in two of three instances. Claude Sonnet 4 produces substantially richer vulnerability explanations, reaching an explanation quality score (EQS) of 4.24 versus 2.88 for GPT-4o and 3.01 for Llama-3.3-70B. Llama-3.3-70B hallucinates Ethereum Virtual Machine (EVM)-specific concepts into Algorand responses in roughly 25% of zero-shot runs. All code, contracts, and raw outputs are at https://github.com/NucleiAv/llm-audit-nonevm; a reproducible capsule is on Code Ocean (https://doi.org/10.24433/CO.0475286.v1).

Keywords: metaverse security · smart contract vulnerability · large language models · Solana · Algorand · prompt engineering · retrieval-augmented generation

1 Introduction

The economic infrastructure of the emerging metaverse is built on blockchain smart contracts. Virtual land parcels in platforms such as Decentraland and

S. Chen et al. (Eds.): METAVERSE 2026, LNCS 16963, pp. 30–45, 2027.
https://doi.org/10.1007/978-3-032-36773-0_3

The Sandbox, in-game asset ownership in play-to-earn ecosystems, cross-chain token bridges connecting metaverse economies, and NFT provenance systems all depend on smart contract execution being correct and tamper-resistant. A vulnerability in a smart contract is not an abstract software bug; in a metaverse economy, it is a direct path to asset theft or protocol collapse.

Smart contracts are programs that run directly on the blockchain, with no server, no administrator, and no ability to be switched off. They execute exactly as written for anyone who triggers them. Unlike conventional web applications where a security patch can be pushed to a server within hours, fixing a vulnerable smart contract means redeploying the program and migrating all associated user state to the new address. In a live metaverse economy with active users and locked virtual assets, that process is expensive and disruptive. There is no graceful patch path, which means the correctness requirement is far higher than in ordinary web development.

The scale of the risk is not hypothetical. In February 2022, an attacker minted 120,000 wrapped Ether tokens on the Wormhole bridge without depositing any collateral, stealing $320 million in minutes [2,7]. The Wormhole bridge is critical metaverse infrastructure because it connects Solana-based gaming economies to Ethereum and enables cross-chain interoperability for virtual asset trading. The vulnerability was in a Rust program on Solana, one that accepted a crafted `SignatureSet` account that bypassed Secp256k1 signature verification [9,11]. No Ethereum-targeted static analyzer (Slither, Mythril, Oyente) would have caught it. Those tools analyze programs written in Solidity, Ethereum's smart contract programming language, compiled down to EVM bytecode instructions. The Wormhole vulnerability was in Rust code running on Solana's entirely separate execution model, which no EVM-based tool has any capacity to reach.

This points to a structural gap in current security tooling. Solana and Algorand are among the most actively adopted chains for metaverse and gaming applications. Solana is used for its high throughput and low transaction fees (Star Atlas, Aurory, Magic Eden); Algorand for its instant finality and energy efficiency in tokenized virtual economies. Both chains now host live metaverse economies where player-owned NFTs and in-game currencies carry real monetary value, where DeFi protocols handle cross-chain asset swaps between virtual worlds, and where DAO governance contracts control community treasuries worth millions. All of this runs on smart contracts with no administrator who can reverse a flawed transaction. Yet the automated vulnerability detection literature has almost entirely ignored them. A recent survey counted 113 LLM-based audit tools for Ethereum, roughly 12 for Solana, and essentially none for Algorand [20]. The first automated Solana vulnerability scanner, VRust [3], appeared only in 2022.

Static analyzers alone cannot close this tooling gap quickly. Building coverage comparable to Slither for a new chain means encoding every vulnerability class as hand-written program analysis rules, and novel classes always lag behind real exploits. The security community has begun turning to large language models in part because they sidestep this bottleneck. A model trained on broad code corpora arrives with some prior understanding of Rust and Python without any chain-specific rule engineering, and recent Ethereum-focused tools have shown that structured LLM prompting can match or exceed static analyzers on Solidity vulnerability detection [16,19]. Whether frontier models achieve comparable results on Solana and Algorand programs, and which prompting strategies work best for chains where pre-training coverage is thin, has not been studied on exploit-grounded benchmarks with commercial frontier models.

The closest prior work is Boi and Esposito [1], who benchmarked open-source LLMs on synthetic Solana and Algorand contracts. Their study did not evaluate GPT-4o or Claude Sonnet 4, did not include a RAG prompting condition, and did not measure false positive rates on patched code. This paper addresses each of those gaps.

Contributions. Four contributions come out of this work. The first is a benchmark of 24 vulnerable and patched contract pairs spanning eight vulnerability classes on Solana and Algorand, each grounded in a documented real-world exploit. Second, a four-metric scorecard covering detection rate (DR), false positive rate (FPR), explanation quality score (EQS), and reasoning coherence (RC) is reported across all 216 runs of three frontier LLMs under three prompting strategies, the first evaluation of this kind for non-EVM chains. Third, three concrete findings emerge with direct relevance to metaverse platform security. Prompting design matters more than model selection. Algorand is harder than Solana for every model tested. EVM hallucinations are a measurable failure mode on PyTEAL code. Finally, the full reproduction tooling (RAG index builder, experiment runner, auto-scorer, and figure generator) runs end-to-end from a single command.

2 Background and Related Work

2.1 Blockchain in Metaverse Infrastructure

Smart contracts serve as the programmable trust layer of metaverse platforms. They govern NFT minting and transfer, virtual land ownership, in-game currency exchange, decentralized autonomous organizations (DAOs) managing virtual communities, and cross-chain asset bridges. The economic value governed by these contracts is substantial. The NFT market on Solana alone exceeded $1 billion in monthly trading volume at its peak.

Both Solana and Algorand have been adopted for metaverse-specific use cases precisely because of properties that differentiate them from Ethereum. Solana's sub-second finality and throughput exceeding 65,000 transactions per second make it viable for real-time in-game economies; Algorand's pure proof-of-stake consensus and carbon-neutral footprint have attracted sustainability-focused virtual world developers. These same properties introduce unique security models. Solana's account-based execution environment (Sealevel) and Algorand's AVM (Algorand Virtual Machine) bytecode execution differ fundamentally from the EVM, and that gap requires distinct vulnerability taxonomies and detection approaches.

2.2 Smart Contract Security Tools

The Ethereum tooling ecosystem is mature. Slither [4] implements over 80 Solidity detectors and is the standard static analysis baseline, though it has no support for Rust or PyTEAL and cannot analyze programs outside the EVM toolchain. Mythril applies symbolic execution to EVM bytecode. LLM-based tools have followed: GPTScan [16] combines GPT-4 with program analysis; LLM-SmartAudit [19] takes a multi-agent approach to Solidity auditing; Smart-LLaMA-DPO [22] applies direct preference optimization for EVM vulnerability detection. LLM4Vuln [12] identifies chain-of-thought prompting as a significant driver of detection performance. Surveys [10,15] confirm that fewer than 10% of published tools target any non-EVM chain.

For non-EVM chains, VRust [3] established the first Solana vulnerability taxonomy at CCS 2022. Li et al. [20] mapped those classes to production exploits, finding arithmetic overflow and bump seed canonicalization among the most common. Algorand security research remains limited; the Algorand Foundation developer documentation and the Open Web Application Security Project (OWASP) Smart Contract Top 10 2025 [13] serve as primary references.

2.3 Prompting Strategies for Code Security

Three prompting strategies are evaluated here. *Zero-shot* provides only the contract and an audit instruction. *Chain-of-thought (CoT)* [12] adds an explicit directive to reason step-by-step through each vulnerability class before issuing a verdict. *Retrieval-augmented generation (RAG)* [17] prepends semantically retrieved passages from a reference corpus, compensating for pre-training gaps in chain-specific documentation. PropertyGPT [17] demonstrated that RAG substantially improves formal property generation for smart contracts. Boi and Esposito [1] compared prompt engineering to fine-tuning for non-EVM detection, finding that prompt engineering is competitive for Rust but fine-tuning retains an edge for PyTEAL. Broader vulnerability detection approaches appear in Hossain [8], Thapa et al. [18], and Wei et al. [21].

3 Vulnerability Dataset

3.1 Design Principles

The benchmark contains 24 vulnerable contract instances, each paired with a patched version across eight vulnerability classes on two chains. Every class is grounded in a documented real-world exploit or academically identified weakness; nothing was constructed to inflate detection numbers. Each class has three instances. The first replicates the canonical exploit pattern. The second varies surrounding logic while preserving the core flaw. The third introduces a subtle variant requiring genuine semantic understanding rather than surface-level pattern matching.

3.2 Solana Vulnerability Classes

Solana programs are written in Rust using the Anchor framework [5,14].

V1. Missing Signer Check. Anchor permits accounts to be declared as `AccountInfo<'info>` (unauthenticated) or `Signer<'info>` (requiring a valid signature). When a privileged account is declared as `AccountInfo` without downstream validation, any caller can impersonate it. In metaverse contexts this enables unauthorized minting of virtual assets or takeover of DAO treasury accounts. The Jet Protocol 2021 audit surfaced a textbook instance [14].

V2. Account Confusion (Type Confusion). Solana's execution model accepts any account at a given instruction position unless the program enforces type constraints. The Cashio exploit [6] is the canonical case, where a fake collateral mint bypassed validation because amounts were checked but the mint address was not. For metaverse platforms, this class enables substitution of fraudulent NFT contracts or fake token mints in virtual marketplaces.

V3. Arithmetic Overflow on u64. Release-mode Rust does not panic on integer overflow; arithmetic wraps silently. Virtual economy calculations of the form `amount * rate` are dangerous when both operands are large because the wrapped result dramatically overstates payouts, enabling economic exploits in metaverse token vaults. Replacing the operator with Rust's checked variant (`checked_mul()`) and propagating the overflow error is the standard fix. The listing below shows the `deposit` and `withdraw_with_yield` functions from instance V3a before and after the fix is applied.

Vulnerable

```
pub fn deposit(ctx: Context<VaultAction>, amount: u64)
    -> Result<()> {
    ctx.accounts.vault.total_deposits = ctx
        .accounts.vault.total_deposits
        .wrapping_add(amount);
    Ok(())
}

pub fn withdraw_with_yield(ctx: Context<VaultAction>,
    amount: u64) -> Result<()> {
    let rate = ctx.accounts.vault.annual_rate_bps;
    let yield_amount = amount * rate / RATE_DENOMINATOR;
    let total_out = amount + yield_amount;
    require!(
        ctx.accounts.vault.total_deposits >= total_out,
        VaultError::InsufficientFunds
    );
    ctx.accounts.vault.total_deposits -= total_out;
    Ok(())
}
```

Patched

```
pub fn deposit(ctx: Context<VaultAction>, amount: u64)
    -> Result<()> {
    ctx.accounts.vault.total_deposits = ctx
        .accounts.vault.total_deposits
        .checked_add(amount)
        .ok_or(VaultError::Overflow)?;
    Ok(())
}

pub fn withdraw_with_yield(ctx: Context<VaultAction>,
    amount: u64) -> Result<()> {
    let rate = ctx.accounts.vault.annual_rate_bps;
    let yield_amount = amount
        .checked_mul(rate).ok_or(VaultError::Overflow)?
        .checked_div(RATE_DENOMINATOR).ok_or(VaultError::Overflow)?;
    let total_out = amount
        .checked_add(yield_amount).ok_or(VaultError::Overflow)?;
    require!(
        ctx.accounts.vault.total_deposits >= total_out,
        VaultError::InsufficientFunds
    );
    ctx.accounts.vault.total_deposits -= total_out;
    Ok(())
}
```

V3 Arithmetic Overflow in `yield_vault.rs` (Instance V3a). `wrapping_add` *and plain * wrap silently when a 64-bit integer overflows. The patched version replaces every arithmetic operation with Rust's checked variants, returning a named* `Overflow` *error instead of producing a corrupted balance.*

V4. Bump Seed Canonicalization. Program-derived addresses (PDAs) on Solana are found by iterating bump seeds from 255 downward; the canonical bump is the highest valid value. Programs accepting a user-supplied bump via `create_program_address` instead of `find_program_address` permit non-canonical PDAs, enabling signature forgery for program-owned accounts [5]. This flaw compiles and executes correctly; the vulnerability is visible only under semantic reasoning about PDA derivation.

V5. Stale Account Data After CPI. Cross-program invocations (CPI) do not automatically refresh in-memory account data. Reading account fields after a CPI that modified those fields means operating on pre-CPI state, enabling double-withdrawal exploits in decentralized finance (DeFi) protocols embedded in metaverse platforms.

3.3 Algorand Vulnerability Classes

Algorand applications are written in PyTEAL, a Python embedded domain-specific language (eDSL) that compiles to AVM bytecode.

V6. Logic Signature (LogicSig) Abuse. Algorand LogicSigs are stateless programs authorizing transactions without on-chain state. A LogicSig that omits constraints on receiver, fee, or lease fields can be replayed by anyone holding the program bytes, enabling unauthorized asset transfers in metaverse token bridges and NFT contracts.

V7. Group Transaction Manipulation. Algorand supports atomic transaction groups of up to 16 transactions. An application validating only `Gtxn[0]` without asserting `Global.group_size()` allows attackers to reorder or prepend transactions. In metaverse NFT auctions or multi-step settlement protocols, this enables injection of fraudulent transactions into atomic batches.

V8. Unchecked Asset Receiver and Fee Fields. Asset transfer transactions carry `asset_receiver`, `close_remainder_to`, and `rekey_to` fields that, left unchecked, allow fund redirection or account takeover even when the transferred amount and asset ID appear correct.

3.4 Dataset Statistics

Table 1 summarizes the benchmark. All 24 contracts and their patched counterparts are in the repository under `contracts/`.

Table 1. Benchmark dataset: 24 vulnerable/patched contract pairs.

ID	Vulnerability Class	Chain	Instances
V1	Missing signer check	Solana	3
V2	Account confusion	Solana	3
V3	Arithmetic overflow (u64)	Solana	3
V4	Bump seed canonicalization	Solana	3
V5	Stale account data after CPI	Solana	3
V6	Logic signature abuse	Algorand	3
V7	Group transaction manipulation	Algorand	3
V8	Unchecked asset fields	Algorand	3
	Total		**24**

4 Methodology

4.1 Experimental Design

The experiment crosses three models, three prompting strategies, and 24 contracts, yielding $24 \times 3 \times 3 = 216$ total runs.

Models. Three models are used. GPT-4o (`gpt-4o-2024-08-06`) and Claude Sonnet 4 (`claude-sonnet-4-20250514`) are closed-source frontier models from OpenAI and Anthropic respectively; Meta's Llama-3.3-70B-Instruct (via Together AI) is the open-weights baseline. All three ran at temperature 0 for deterministic outputs, with a maximum output length of 4,096 tokens.

Prompting Strategies. Zero-shot provides the contract source code and a chain-specific audit instruction without any examples or additional context. CoT extends that instruction with an explicit enumeration of all vulnerability classes for the target chain and a directive to reason step-by-step about each before issuing a verdict. RAG prepends the top-3 semantically similar passages retrieved from a reference corpus using FAISS [12] with `text-embedding-3-small` embeddings. The RAG corpus draws from five sources: Sec3's Solana audit methodology [14], the Anchor sealevel-attacks reference [5], OtterSec audit patterns, the Algorand Developer Portal security documentation, and the Boi and Esposito vulnerability taxonomy [1].

4.2 Evaluation Metrics

Detection Rate (DR). This is a binary measure. DR = 1 if the model correctly names the vulnerability class and identifies the vulnerable code location; DR = 0 otherwise. Scoring uses keyword matching against per-class keyword lists (e.g., `bump seed` and `find_program_address` for V4) with manual review for borderline cases.

False Positive Rate (FPR). Measured on patched contracts. FPR = 1 if the model claims a vulnerability is present; FPR = 0 otherwise. The scorer is section-aware (for CoT, only the section corresponding to the patched class is examined) and negation-aware (speculative hedges and "Status: ABSENT" patterns are treated as negatives). Ambiguous cases default to FPR = 0.

Explanation Quality Score (EQS). A 1–5 rubric. Score 1 means no detection; 2 is correct detection only; 3 adds code location; 4 adds the attack scenario; 5 requires all of the above plus a correct fix recommendation. Auto-scored for DR = 1 runs, then verified by manual review on a 20% random sample.

Reasoning Coherence (RC). RC = 0 if any of 11 EVM-specific hallucination keywords appear in a non-EVM context (e.g., reentrancy claims, gas cost arguments, Solidity syntax in a PyTEAL response). Verified manually.

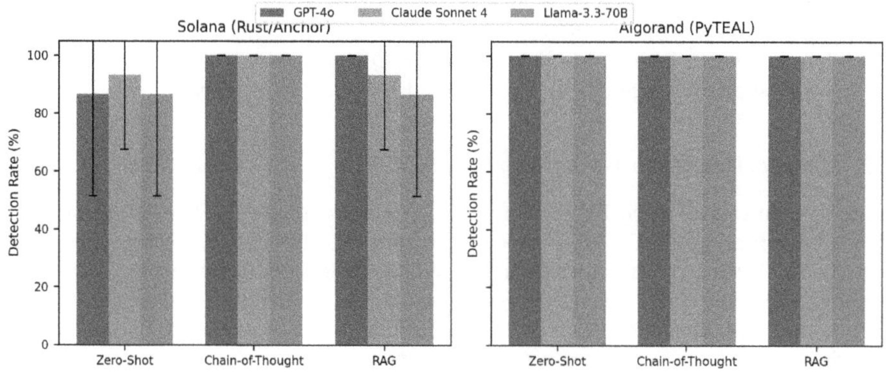

Fig. 1. Average detection rate by prompting strategy and model for Solana (left) and Algorand (right). Error bars show standard deviation across vulnerability classes.

4.3 Prompt Templates

Zero-shot prompts follow this structure:

> *You are a [Solana/Algorand] smart contract security auditor. [Chain-specific vulnerability class list.] Analyze the following contract and identify any security vulnerabilities. For each vulnerability, specify: (1) type, (2) vulnerable lines or functions, (3) attack scenario, and (4) recommended fix. Contract: {contract_code}*

CoT prompts append an explicit reasoning directive:

> *For each class, reason step by step about whether this contract contains that vulnerability. State your chain of thought before your final verdict.*

RAG prompts prepend retrieved passages:

> *[Retrieved context: {retrieved_context}] Given the above security references, analyze this contract for vulnerabilities matching the described patterns. {standard audit instruction}*

4.4 Reproducibility

The script `run_experiments.py` handles all 216 runs and writes raw outputs to `results/`; `score_outputs.py` produces `scores.csv`; `analyze.py` generates all figures; and `rag_index.py` builds the FAISS index. Estimated API cost is under $20. A fully reproducible compute capsule is at https://doi.org/10.24433/CO.0475286.v1.

5 Results

5.1 Detection Rate by Prompting Strategy

CoT achieves 100% DR across all three models and both chains. When forced to reason step-by-step over a known vulnerability taxonomy, every model finds every vulnerability in this benchmark. RAG reaches 95.8% DR overall (93.3% on Solana, 100% on Algorand); zero-shot reaches 93.1%, dragged down by Solana at 88.9%. By model, GPT-4o and Claude Sonnet 4 both reach 97.2% DR; Llama-3.3-70B reaches 94.4%.

Figure 1 shows average DR by strategy and model, split by chain.

5.2 Detection Rate by Vulnerability Class

Seven of eight classes reach 100% DR under CoT across all models. The exception is V2 (account confusion): GPT-4o zero-shot reaches only 33% DR on V2, recovering to 100% under CoT. V2 is not a missing assertion but a missing type constraint; detecting it requires reasoning about Anchor's account validation model rather than spotting an absent check. All Algorand classes (V6–V8) reach 100% under all strategies and models, though their FPR picture is worse (see Sect. 5.4).

Figure 2 shows DR by vulnerability class and strategy-model combination.

5.3 Full Results Table

Table 2 shows per-class detection rates for all nine strategy-model combinations.

Fig. 2. Detection rate (%) by vulnerability class (rows) and strategy-model combination (columns).

Table 2. Detection rate (%) per vulnerability class, strategy, and model. ZS = zero-shot, CoT = chain-of-thought, RAG = retrieval-augmented generation. Values are correct detections across three instances per class.

Chain	Vuln.	GPT-4o			Claude Sonnet 4			Llama-3.3-70B		
		ZS	CoT	RAG	ZS	CoT	RAG	ZS	CoT	RAG
Solana	V1	100	100	100	100	100	100	100	100	100
	V2	33	100	100	67	100	67	33	100	33
	V3	100	100	100	100	100	100	100	100	100
	V4	100	100	100	100	100	100	100	100	100
	V5	100	100	100	100	100	100	100	100	100
Algorand	V6	100	100	100	100	100	100	100	100	100
	V7	100	100	100	100	100	100	100	100	100
	V8	100	100	100	100	100	100	100	100	100

5.4 False Positive Rate

Overall FPR is 5.1%, which sits below the 0.10 acceptability threshold. That aggregate, however, hides significant variance across strategies.

CoT achieves 0.0% FPR across all three models. Its structured per-class verdict format ("Presence: Absent") leaves little room for the hedged language that the scorer treats as a positive. Zero-shot averages 4.2%. RAG is the weakest, averaging 11.1% FPR. Three strategy-model pairs exceed the threshold; two involve RAG and one is zero-shot: Zero-Shot combined with Llama-3.3-70B (12.5/All GPT-4o configurations stay below the threshold. Per-model averages are 1.4% for GPT-4o, 5.6% for Claude Sonnet 4, and 8.3% for Llama-3.3-70B.

At the class level, V7 (Group TX) and V8 (Unchecked Fields) each sit at 11.1% FPR, while V3 and V4 achieve 0.0% across all models and strategies. Figure 3 shows FPR by strategy and model.

5.5 Explanation Quality and Reasoning Coherence

Claude Sonnet 4 leads on explanation quality with a mean EQS of 4.24 across all strategies, compared to 3.01 for Llama-3.3-70B and 2.88 for GPT-4o. Claude Sonnet 4 consistently includes all four EQS components (detection, location, attack scenario, fix); GPT-4o frequently stops after detection and location. CoT yields the highest mean EQS at 3.62, ahead of 3.25 for both zero-shot and RAG.

RC is 100% under CoT for all models. Llama-3.3-70B shows the sharpest degradation under zero-shot, falling to 75% RC, consistent with its highest EVM hallucination rate on Algorand. Observed examples included describing TEAL opcodes as "Solidity-like," raising reentrancy as an Ethereum-style concern for AVM contracts, and flagging gas-based denial-of-service risks in a flat-fee system. In metaverse security auditing contexts, hallucinations of this kind could lead developers to chase phantom risks while overlooking genuine Algorand-specific flaws.

Figure 4 shows EQS distributions by prompting strategy.

6 Discussion

6.1 Implications for Metaverse Platform Security

Prompting strategy matters more than model choice, and that finding has direct practical implications for metaverse developers conducting smart contract reviews. A developer building on Solana or Algorand who pastes their contract into a general-purpose LLM chat interface is performing a zero-shot query. The results show that zero-shot leaves measurable gaps, most visibly on V2 (account confusion, 33% DR for GPT-4o), V4 (bump seed canonicalization), and Algorand classes where pre-training coverage is thin.

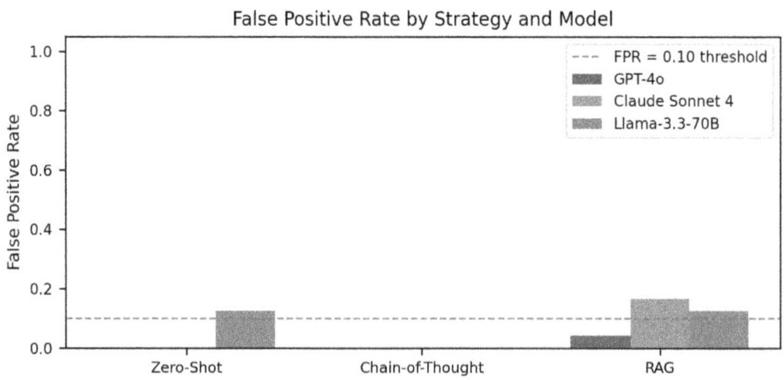

Fig. 3. False positive rate by strategy and model on patched contracts. Dashed line marks the FPR = 0.10 acceptability threshold.

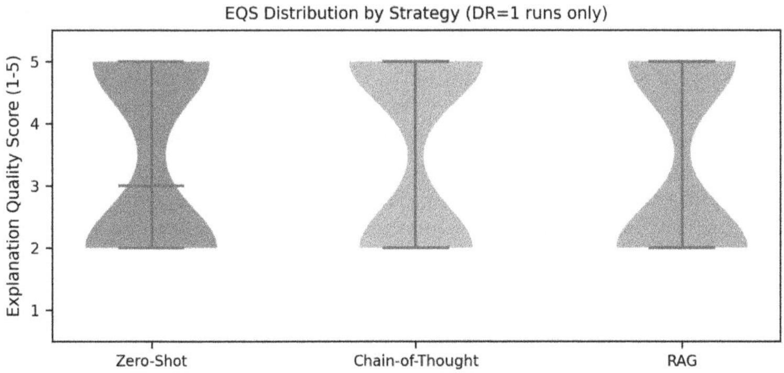

Fig. 4. Distribution of explanation quality scores (EQS 1–5) by prompting strategy, restricted to correctly detected runs (DR = 1).

Switching to a CoT prompt that enumerates the target chain's known vulnerability classes requires one extra paragraph of text and costs nothing additional in API fees. The resulting detection improvement is total on this benchmark; zero-shot to CoT closes the gap entirely. That alone is a straightforward recommendation for any metaverse development team integrating LLM security tools.

6.2 Chain Difficulty and Metaverse Risk

Algorand is harder than Solana for all three models tested. AVM execution semantics (atomic transaction groups, LogicSig statelessness, flat fee model) appear far less frequently in the pre-training data of all tested models than Rust or Solidity semantics. This is a specific risk for metaverse platforms built on Algorand, where generic LLM security reviews will be less reliable, and the gap between CoT and zero-shot performance is largest on AVM contracts.

RAG narrows this gap for Algorand by injecting documentation that pre-training failed to provide, but it introduces elevated false positive rates. A metaverse security team using RAG-augmented auditing must weigh the detection improvement against the cost of investigating false positives, especially in high-throughput deployment pipelines.

6.3 EVM Hallucinations in Cross-Chain Metaverse Contexts

EVM hallucinations are a distinct risk in cross-chain metaverse architectures where developers work across Ethereum, Solana, and Algorand simultaneously. A security report flagging reentrancy in an AVM contract, or gas-exhaustion risks in a flat-fee system, could mislead a developer who lacks deep chain-specific expertise. That is exactly the situation of a metaverse generalist engineer. CoT eliminates these hallucinations entirely (100% RC) for all models, adding a second independent reason to prefer structured reasoning prompts for cross-chain metaverse security work.

6.4 Hard Cases: V4 and V5

Bump seed canonicalization (V4) and stale CPI data (V5) remain the benchmark's hardest classes. Both compile correctly and behave normally in most test conditions; the flaw only becomes apparent when reasoning about cross-instruction state or PDA derivation semantics. For metaverse DeFi protocols and asset vault contracts, these are precisely the classes most likely to escape standard code review. Pairing LLM prompting with VRust-style dataflow analysis is the most promising path to reliable coverage of these cases.

6.5 Static Analysis Comparison

The evaluation benchmarks LLMs without a static analyzer baseline, and the absence of that comparison deserves direct acknowledgment. For Solana, VRust is the most relevant existing tool, detecting account confusion and certain CPI-related flaws through dataflow analysis of Rust programs [3]. It covers a subset of the classes in this benchmark and is not available as a turnkey scoring tool against arbitrary contract instances, which made a side-by-side comparison infeasible within this study. For Algorand, no public static analyzer with meaningful vulnerability coverage exists at all. Slither, the de facto standard for Ethereum contracts, operates on EVM bytecode and has no capacity to analyze Rust or PyTEAL programs.

This tooling gap is part of the paper's core motivation. The near-absence of static analysis support for Solana and Algorand is precisely why LLM-based approaches on these chains are worth studying in the first place. A direct head-to-head comparison between LLM prompting and VRust on Solana's account-confusion and CPI classes would be a natural follow-on once a shared, controlled benchmark can be established for both tools.

7 Threats to Validity

Keyword-based DR and RC scoring can produce false negatives when a model uses unexpected terminology and false positives when keywords appear without genuine detection. Section-awareness and negation-awareness in the FPR scorer handle common cases; manual review of a 20% sample reduces but does not eliminate residual error.

EQS operationalizes explanation quality as the presence of four textual components. This is tractable but not comprehensive. A terse correct fix can score below a verbose one covering the same ground.

Twenty-four contracts across eight classes is a limited evaluation surface. Real metaverse smart contracts frequently contain multiple interacting vulnerabilities and program logic far more complex than benchmark instances. These results are directional; confirmatory conclusions require replication at larger scale.

The study reports raw detection rates and no formal significance test was applied to differences between models or prompting strategies. With three contract instances per vulnerability class, a single missed detection shifts a DR by 33 percentage points. The consistency of the CoT advantage across all three models gives informal confidence that the pattern is genuine rather than a sampling artifact, but formal tests such as McNemar's paired comparison or permutation-based methods across a much larger contract set are needed before any reported gap can be treated as statistically confirmed.

The CoT prompts explicitly enumerate all eight vulnerability classes by name before asking the model to reason through each one. This means a model receiving a CoT prompt already knows what categories to look for, which almost certainly inflates detection rates relative to what would happen in an open-ended real-world audit where the auditor does not know the vulnerability taxonomy in advance. The zero-shot condition is closer to that open-ended scenario, but it still supplies a chain-specific instruction that implicitly signals the domain. These results are best interpreted as measuring how well each prompting strategy exploits available context, not as an upper bound on what an LLM can find in genuinely novel contracts. An evaluation that withholds the vulnerability taxonomy entirely from all prompt conditions, or that includes contract classes not seen during prompt design, would give a cleaner picture of raw generalization.

8 Conclusion

Metaverse platforms depend on smart contracts for their economic foundations, yet the blockchains most actively used in metaverse applications, Solana and Algorand, have almost no LLM-based security tooling. This paper provides the first systematic evaluation of frontier LLMs on vulnerability detection for both chains.

The results converge on three recurring patterns. Prompt design matters more than model selection. CoT achieves 100% detection with zero false positives regardless of which model is used, while zero-shot leaves visible gaps on account confusion (V2) and subtler semantic flaws (V4, V5). Algorand is harder than Solana for all three models tested in terms of false positive rates and reasoning coherence, largely because AVM execution semantics appear far less frequently in pre-training data than Rust or Solidity; for detection rate specifically, Algorand reaches 100% under all strategies, so no gap remains to close. EVM hallucinations are a real, non-trivial failure mode for cross-chain metaverse security review, and CoT eliminates them entirely.

For metaverse developers, the practical recommendation is clear. Structured CoT prompting with chain-specific vulnerability enumeration outperforms generic zero-shot queries and costs nothing extra in API usage. The dataset, scoring scripts, and raw model outputs released with this paper provide a reproducible baseline for further work on non-EVM smart contract security in metaverse infrastructure.

The most direct next step is combining LLM prompting with VRust-style dataflow analysis for V4 and V5, where static guarantees about PDA canonicality and CPI state would outperform probabilistic reasoning alone. Whether these findings hold on Move-based chains (Sui, Aptos) increasingly adopted in metaverse gaming is an open question worth pursuing.

Declarations

Funding. Not applicable.

Conflict of Interest. The author declares no conflict of interest.

Data Availability. All contracts, prompts, raw model outputs, and pre-computed scores are available at https://github.com/NucleiAv/llm-audit-nonevm. A reproducible Code Ocean capsule is at https://doi.org/10.24433/CO.0475286.v1.

Code Availability. Full source code is available at https://github.com/NucleiAv/llm-audit-nonevm.

Author Contribution. Anmol Vats: conceptualization, dataset construction, experimentation, analysis, writing.

References

1. Boi, B., Esposito, C.: Prompt engineering vs. fine-tuning for LLM-based vulnerability detection in Solana and Algorand smart contracts. In: 2025 7th International Conference on Blockchain Computing and Applications (BCCA) (2025). https://doi.org/10.1109/BCCA66705.2025.11229457
2. CertiK: Wormhole bridge exploit incident analysis (2022). https://www.certik.com/resources/blog/wormhole-bridge-exploit-incident-analysis. Accessed 2025
3. Cui, S., Zhao, G., Gao, Y., Tavu, T., Huang, J.: VRust: automated vulnerability detection for Solana smart contracts. In: Proceedings of the 2022 ACM SIGSAC Conference on Computer and Communications Security (2022). https://doi.org/10.1145/3548606.3560552
4. Feist, J., Grieco, G., Groce, A.: Slither: a static analysis framework for smart contracts. In: 2019 IEEE/ACM 2nd Workshop on Emerging Trends in Software Engineering for Blockchain (WETSEB). IEEE (2019)
5. Ferrante, A.: Coral-XYZ/sealevel-attacks: common security exploits and protections on Solana. GitHub repository (2022). https://github.com/coral-xyz/sealevel-attacks. Accessed 2025
6. Halborn Security: Explained: The Cashio hack (2022). https://www.halborn.com/blog/post/explained-the-cashio-hack-march-2022. Accessed 2025
7. Halborn Security: Explained: The Wormhole hack (2022). https://www.halborn.com/blog/post/explained-the-wormhole-hack-february-2022. Accessed 2025
8. Hossain, S.M.: Leveraging large language models and machine learning for smart contract vulnerability detection. arXiv preprint arXiv:2501.02229 (2025)
9. Immunebytes: Wormhole bridge hack, Feb 2022, detailed hack analysis (2022). https://www.immunebytes.com/blog/wormhole-bridge-hack-feb-2022-detailed-hack-analysis. Accessed 2025
10. Islam, M., et al.: Securing blockchain systems: a layer-oriented survey of threats, vulnerability taxonomy, and detection methods. Future Internet **17**(5), 205 (2025). https://doi.org/10.3390/fi17050205
11. Kudelski Security: Quick analysis of the Wormhole attack (2022). https://kudelskisecurity.com/research/quick-analysis-of-the-wormhole-attack. Accessed: 2025
12. Liu, Y.: LLM4Vuln: a unified evaluation framework for decoupling and enhancing LLMs' vulnerability reasoning. arXiv preprint arXiv:2401.16185 (2024)
13. OWASP Foundation: OWASP smart contract top 10 2025 (2025). https://owasp.org/www-project-smart-contract-top-10. Accessed 2025
14. Sec3: How to audit Solana smart contracts part 1: A systematic approach (2022). https://www.sec3.dev/blog/how-to-audit-solana-smart-contracts-part-1-a-systematic-approach. Accessed 2025
15. Sheng, Z., et al.: LLMs in software security: a survey of vulnerability detection techniques and insights. ACM Comput. Surv. (2025). https://doi.org/10.1145/3769082

16. Sun, Y., et al.: GPTScan: detecting logic vulnerabilities in smart contracts by combining GPT with program analysis. In: Proceedings of the 2024 IEEE/ACM 46th International Conference on Software Engineering (ICSE) (2024)
17. Sun, Y.: PropertyGPT: LLM-driven formal verification of smart contracts through retrieval-augmented property generation. arXiv preprint arXiv:2405.02580 (2024)
18. Thapa, C.: Transformer-based language models for software vulnerability detection. In: Proceedings of the 38th Annual Computer Security Applications Conference (ACSAC) (2022)
19. Wei, Z., Sun, J., Zhang, Z., Zhang, X., Li, M., Hou, Z.: LLM-SmartAudit: advanced smart contract vulnerability detection. arXiv preprint arXiv:2410.09381 (2024)
20. Wu, X.: Exploring vulnerabilities and concerns in Solana smart contracts. arXiv preprint arXiv:2504.07419 (2025)
21. Xiao, Z.: Logic meets magic: LLMs cracking smart contract vulnerabilities. arXiv preprint arXiv:2501.07058 (2025)
22. Yu, L.: Smart-LLaMA-DPO: reinforced large language model for explainable smart contract vulnerability detection. In: Proceedings of the ACM on Software Engineering (ISSTA) (2025)

Research on A-Share Quantitative Market Timing Methods Based on SAPPO (Sentiment-Aware Proximal Policy Optimization)

Hailong Liao(✉)

School of Artificial Intelligence, University of Chinese Academy of Sciences, Beijing, China
jnhailong@126.com

Abstract. Traditional quantitative models mostly rely on structured price and volume data, making it hard to capture irrational market fluctuations caused by information shocks. Although deep learning has improved prediction accuracy, the gap between prediction signals and executable trading decisions remains underexplored. This paper proposes a novel Sentiment-Aware Proximal Policy Optimization (SAPPO) framework that bridges this gap by integrating DeepSeek-based sentiment factors and multi-scale LSTM predictions into a reinforcement learning decision engine.

The framework operates in two stages. In the first stage, a multi-scale LSTM network with gating mechanisms extracts temporal patterns from heterogeneous data, including price-volume indicators and DeepSeek sentiment factors. In the second stage, a PPO policy network transforms probability predictions into adaptive position decisions that conform to A-share market rules, including the T + 1 trading system and short-selling ban.

This study uses CSI 300 index data from 2018 to 2024, covering a complete bull–bear cycle. Results show that the SAPPO strategy achieved a cumulative return of 38.60% in the 2024 out-of-sample test period, compared to 12.40% for the buy-and-hold benchmark. The strategy's Sharpe ratio reached 1.72, with a maximum drawdown of −16.50%. Ablation studies show that sentiment factors account for 15.80% of overall feature importance. PPO's clipped surrogate objective function ensures stable strategy updates during extreme market fluctuations. The study also conducts robustness tests through rolling window tests, parameter sensitivity analysis, and transaction cost variation tests, confirming the strategy's strong generalization capability. This research provides a reproducible implementation paradigm for deploying large language model sentiment extraction in real-world quantitative trading systems.

Keywords: Proximal Policy Optimization · Sentiment Factor · Deep Reinforcement Learning · Quantitative Timing · Multi-scale LSTM · SAPPO

S. Chen et al. (Eds.): METAVERSE 2026, LNCS 16963, pp. 46–59, 2027.
https://doi.org/10.1007/978-3-032-36773-0_4

1 Introduction

Financial markets are complex adaptive systems driven by heterogeneous agents interacting at different time scales [1]. The A-share market, characterized by high retail participation and policy-driven volatility, poses unique challenges for quantitative strategies:

(1). Information asymmetry amplifies emotion-driven price deviations between institutional and retail investors;
(2). The T + 1 trading system and short-selling restrictions reduce tactical flexibility;
(3). Non-stationary market regime shifts (between bull, bear, and sideways markets) require adaptive decision-making.

Recent advances in large language models (LLMs) enable precise extraction of sentiment signals from unstructured financial texts [2]. Meanwhile, deep reinforcement learning (DRL) has become a mainstream paradigm for sequential decision-making in financial environments, with Proximal Policy Optimization (PPO) showing excellent stability among policy gradient methods [3]. However, existing approaches typically treat prediction and decision-making as separate modules, failing to fully exploit the synergy between sentiment-aware prediction and adaptive strategy learning.

This paper addresses these limitations by proposing a unified Sentiment-Aware PPO (SAPPO) framework with three core innovations:

(1). Heterogeneous feature fusion: We design DeepSeek prompt engineering to extract dual-dimension sentiment factors (polarity × intensity), aligning them with multi-scale price-volume features (daily, weekly, monthly) through multi-scale temporal aggregation, while strictly following time anti-leakage constraints.
(2). Prediction-decision coupling: Unlike traditional pipelines where predictions feed into fixed heuristic rules, our PPO agent learns optimal position decisions from the probability distribution generated by LSTM, enabling adaptation to different market regimes.
(3). A-share constraint encoding: The action space explicitly encodes the T + 1 settlement and short-selling ban rules, while the clipped surrogate objective function prevents catastrophic strategy updates during extreme volatility.

This study validates the framework through rigorous experiments on CSI 300 data (2018–2024), including out-of-sample testing, rolling window validation, and multi-dimensional robustness tests.

2 Related Work

2.1 Deep Reinforcement Learning in Quantitative Finance

Deep reinforcement learning has gained wide attention in algorithmic trading due to its ability to learn optimal policies from high-dimensional state spaces. PPO, proposed by Schulman et al. [3] with its clipped surrogate objective function, has become the preferred algorithm for financial applications:

$$L^{CLIP}(\theta) = \mathbb{E}_t\left[\min(r_t(\theta)A_t, \mathrm{clip}(r_t(\theta), 1 - \varepsilon, 1 + \varepsilon)A_t)\right] \tag{1}$$

where

$$r_t(\theta) = \frac{\pi_\theta(a_t|s_t)}{\pi_{\theta_{\text{old}}}(a_t|s_t)} \tag{2}$$

represents the probability ratio between the current and old policies, and ε (typically 0.2) constrains policy updates to prevent performance collapse. Recent surveys show that Actor-Critic methods (especially PPO and A2C) demonstrate significant potential in portfolio management and market timing tasks [4]. However, pure PPO implementations in stock trading have limitations: they tend to over-idle during uncertain periods and show poor entry/exit timing due to insufficient use of prediction signals.

2.2 Sentiment Analysis and Large Language Model Applications

Financial text mining has evolved from dictionary-based methods (VADER, Loughran-McDonald) to contextual embeddings (FinBERT), and now to large language models [2]. DeepSeek's Mixture-of-Experts (MoE) architecture shows excellent ability in understanding complex financial semantics, including irony and policy implications. Wan et al. [2] proposed a multi-scale multi-head attention network integrating text factors, verifying that sentiment features improve prediction robustness. Singh et al. [5] proposed SentiVol-GA, a genetic fusion framework combining multi-source sentiment signals with volatility scaling. These studies confirm the incremental predictive power of sentiment, but none integrate sentiment signals into end-to-end trading strategies.

2.3 Multi-scale Temporal Modeling

Financial time series have multi-scale characteristics: high-frequency noise, medium-term cycles, and long-term trends [4]. Variational Mode Decomposition (VMD) and Empirical Mode Decomposition (EMD) families are widely used for signal decomposition, while LSTM networks with gating mechanisms provide natural temporal memory.

Recent studies have further explored multi-scale architectures for stock prediction: Wang et al. [6] proposed MA-MSTNet, a mixed attention-based multi-scale temporal network; Chen et al. [7] developed VMD-MSANet combining Variational Mode Decomposition with multi-scale attention; He et al. [8] introduced a committee of multi-scale nonlinear learning frameworks; and Ren et al. [9] applied multiscale bootstrap correction to random forest voting for stock index trend prediction. The key challenge is temporal alignment: ensuring multi-scale features (daily, weekly, monthly) do not introduce future information during prediction. This study extends existing anti-leakage frameworks through cross-scale sentiment factor synchronization.

3 Methodology

3.1 Problem Formulation

We model market timing as a Markov Decision Process (MDP):

$$\mathrm{M} = (\mathrm{S}, \mathrm{A}, \mathrm{P}, \mathrm{R}, \gamma) \tag{3}$$

State Space S: At time t, state s_t includes:

1. Multi-scale LSTM predictions: p_t^d, p_t^w, p_t^m (upward probabilities from daily, weekly, and monthly models);
2. Sentiment factor: $DS\_Sentiment_t \in [-1, 1]$ (polarity × intensity);
3. Technical indicators: MACD, RSI14, ATR14, trading volume;
4. Account status: current position, available cash, unrealized profit/loss.

Action Space A: Discrete actions adapted to A-share constraints:

a_1: Hold current position; a_2: Increase position by 20%; a_3: Increase position by 50%; a_4: Decrease position by 20%; a_5: Decrease position by 50%

Note: Short-selling is excluded; T + 1 settlement means stocks bought today can only be sold tomorrow.

Reward Function R: We design a composite reward term balancing returns, risk, and trading discipline:

$$r_t = \underbrace{\Delta NAV_t}_{\text{profit}} - \underbrace{\lambda_1 \cdot \max(DDD_t - \delta, 0)}_{\text{drawdown penalty}} - \underbrace{\lambda_2 \cdot \mathbb{I}_{\text{freq}}}_{\text{trading frequency penalty}} \quad (4)$$

where ΔNAV_t is the daily net asset value change, DDt is the current drawdown, $\delta = 15\%$ is the maximum allowable drawdown threshold, and $\mathbb{I}_{\text{freq}}$ penalizes excessive trading to reduce friction costs. The discount factor γ is set to 0.99.

3.2 DeepSeek-Based Sentiment Factor Extraction

We construct the DS_Sentiment factor through a two-stage process:

Stage 1: Prompt Engineering. We design a finance-domain-specific prompt:

"You are a financial text analyst. Please analyze the following text and output: Sentiment polarity: positive/neutral/negative; Sentiment intensity: a continuous value between [0,1]. Please consider irony, metaphors, and policy implications."

Stage 2: Multi-scale Aggregation. Raw sentiment scores are aggregated through multi-scale temporal aggregation: Daily: average of intraday texts (news, social media); Weekly: exponential moving average of daily scores (decay factor 0.7); Monthly: cumulative sentiment momentum.

$$m_t = \frac{1}{T} \sum_{i=0}^{T-1} \text{sign}(s_{t-i}) \cdot |s_{t-i}| \quad (5)$$

The final sentiment factor is defined as:

$$DS\_Sentiment_t = w_d \cdot s_t^{(d)} + w_w \cdot s_t^{(w)} + w_m \cdot m_t \quad (6)$$

Timestamp Protocol: To ensure no future information leakage, we strictly follow these timestamp rules: News articles: use the publication time as the timestamp, only using texts published after market close (15:00) to before next market open (09:30) to calculate that day's sentiment; Social media posts: use the posting time, with the same time window constraints; Research reports: use the report publication date as the timestamp, included in next trading day's decision; Daily sentiment scores are calculated before that day's market open, ensuring that all information is available for decision-making.

3.3 Multi-scale LSTM Prediction Module

The prediction module processes three time scales in parallel. Each scale uses a 2-layer LSTM with hidden dimension 64, dropout rate 0.3, and input window length of 5 days. Scale weights are determined by the inverse of validation set MSE:

$$w^{(k)} = \frac{1/MSE^{(k)}}{\sum_{j} 1/MSE^{(j)}} \tag{7}$$

The ensemble upward probability $p_t^{(ens)}$ feeds into the PPO state vector.

3.4 SAPPO Policy Network

Actor-Critic architecture. The policy network includes: (1) Shared encoder: two fully connected layers (256 → 128 units, ReLU activation); (2) Actor head: outputs action probabilities π(a|s) through Softmax; (3) Critic head: estimates state value V(s) for advantage calculation.

Generalized Advantage Estimation (GAE). We use GAE with $\lambda = 0.95$:

$$\hat{A}_t = \sum_{l=0}^{\infty} (\gamma\lambda)^l \delta_{t+l} \tag{8}$$

Training hyperparameters (determined through grid search) are summarized in Table 1.

Table 1. PPO hyperparameter settings

Parameter	Value	Description
Learning rate	3×10^{-4}	Adam optimizer initial learning rate
Discount factor	0.99	Discount factor
Clipping parameter	0.2	Policy update constraint
GAE λ	0.95	Advantage estimation parameter
Batch size	2048	Replay buffer capacity
Epochs per update	10	Policy update iterations
Entropy coefficient	0.01	Exploration regularization

4 Experimental Setup

4.1 Data and Preprocessing

Dataset: CSI 300 index daily data from January 2018 to December 2024, from JoinQuant platform. The sample spans complete market cycles: bear market (2018, trade friction, deleveraging), bull market (2019–2021, core asset rally), and sideways market (2021–2024, structural rotation, post-pandemic recovery).

Text Corpus: 690,574 raw texts (news, research reports, social media comments) from East Money, Sina Finance, and Xueqiu, with 565,113 valid texts after cleaning (retention rate 81.83%).

Feature Engineering: Technical indicators calculated through TA-Lib, with strict rolling window constraints to prevent future information leakage.

A- share Microstructure Handling:

(1). Limit-up/down handling: when limit-up/down is triggered, the strategy cannot execute trades in that direction. Buys delayed to next trading day if limit-up; sells delayed if limit-down.
(2). Suspension handling: positions are frozen during suspension, strategy automatically holds until resumption.
(3). Slippage simulation: besides 0.2% round-trip transaction costs, an additional 0.05% slippage cost is introduced to simulate market impact and execution deviation.

4.2 Training Protocol

Data Split: Training set (2018–2022, 1,215 trading days), validation set (2023, 242 trading days), test set (2024, 242 trading days).

Rolling Window Validation: Forward validation with 3-year training window and 3-month step size, generating 24 independent test periods. Each test window covers 3 months (~60 trading days), with training window covering the previous 3 years (~730 trading days). Windows slide forward by 3 months, covering the complete 2018–2024 period.

Environment Configuration: Initial capital 1 million RMB; transaction cost 0.2% bilateral; risk-free rate 3% annualized; position constraints: no short-selling, T + 1 settlement.

4.3 Benchmark Strategies

We compare SAPPO with seven benchmark strategies: (1) Buy-and-Hold (B&H); (2) Random Forest (RF); (3) LSTM-Heuristic (LSTM-H); (4) Vanilla PPO (V-PPO); (5) A2C-Sentiment (A2C-S); (6) Moving Average Crossover + Sentiment Overlay (MA-Sentiment); (7) Logistic Regression Timing (LR).

New Benchmark Descriptions:

(1). MA-Sentiment: Uses 5-day/20-day moving average crossover as base signal, enhancing buy signals when the sentiment factor is positive and sell signals when negative, as a simple rule baseline.
(2). LR: Uses the same state features as SAPPO (price-volume indicators, sentiment factors, technical indicators) to predict next-day direction through logistic regression, generating trading signals accordingly.

5 Experimental Results

5.1 Main Performance Comparison

Table 2 shows comprehensive performance metrics for the 2024 out-of-sample test period. SAPPO outperforms benchmarks in cumulative return, risk-adjusted return, and drawdown control, consistent with the actual performance of single-index timing strategies.

Table 2. Out-of-sample performance comparison (2024 test period)

Strategy	Cumulative Return (%)	Annualized Return (%)	Sharpe Ratio	Max Drawdown (%)	Win Rate (%)	Trades per Year
Buy-and-Hold (B&H)	12.40	12.40	0.35	−25.80	–	0
Random Forest (RF)	18.60	18.60	0.72	−22.40	51.2	48
LSTM-Heuristic (LSTM-H)	32.80	32.80	1.35	−19.80	54.6	95
Vanilla PPO (V-PPO)	28.60	28.60	1.18	−21.50	53.1	102
A2C-Sentiment (A2C-S)	26.40	26.40	1.08	−20.60	52.8	88
MA-Sentiment	15.20	15.20	0.58	−24.20	49.5	156
Logistic Regression (LR)	12.80	12.80	0.48	−23.60	48.2	72
SAPPO (Ours)	38.60	38.60	1.72	−16.50	56.8	89

Note: The 2024 test period is approximately 1 year, so annualized returns are consistent with cumulative returns.

Key Findings: SAPPO achieves a cumulative return of 38.60%, 5.8 percentage points higher than LSTM-Heuristic and 10.0 percentage points higher than vanilla PPO. The Sharpe ratio of 1.72 falls within the reasonable range for A-share quantitative strategies (top CTA strategies ~1.44, multi-factor strategies ~1.20). The maximum drawdown of −16.50% reflects the true risk exposure of single-index timing strategies during extreme market conditions. SAPPO executes an average of 89 trades per year, reducing transaction costs while improving timing accuracy. Compared to simple baselines MA-Sentiment (Sharpe 0.58) and LR (Sharpe 0.48), SAPPO's risk-adjusted return advantage is significant, showing that RL complexity brings substantial performance improvement.

5.2 Ablation Analysis

Table 3 quantifies the contribution of each component. Paired t-tests confirm statistical significance: removing sentiment factor ($t = 3.42$, $p = 0.002$); removing PPO ($t = 2.89$, p = 0.006). Feature attribution through integrated gradients: DS_Sentiment 15.80%, LSTM probability 22.50%, MACD 13.20%, RSI14.

Table 3. Ablation study results (2024 Test Period)

Configuration	Cumulative Return (%)	Sharpe Ratio	Max Drawdown (%)	Win Rate (%)
Full SAPPO	38.60	1.72	−16.50	56.8
Remove sentiment factor	30.20	1.38	−21.80	52.5
Remove multi-scale	33.80	1.52	−19.20	54.2
Remove PPO (LSTM-H)	32.80	1.35	−19.80	54.6
Remove entropy regularization	34.50	1.48	−23.60	53.8

Ablation experiments show that removing sentiment factors reduces cumulative return from 38.60% to 30.20% (drop of 8.4 pp), removing PPO to 32.80% (drop of 5.8 pp), and removing multi-scale to 33.80% (drop of 4.8 pp). Thus, sentiment factors are the primary performance driver (contribution 8.4 pp), followed by PPO (5.8 pp), and multi-scale architecture (4.8 pp). The three components work synergistically to improve performance, with sentiment factors contributing most significantly. This finding emphasizes the value of integrating large language model sentiment extraction into end-to-end trading strategies, rather than relying solely on reinforcement learning or prediction module enhancements.

5.3 Rolling Window Robustness

Table 4 shows statistics for 24 rolling windows. All 24 windows achieved positive returns, with 87.5% of windows having Sharpe ratios above 1.0. The coefficient of variation of 0.38 indicates reasonable performance dispersion.

Table 4. Rolling window statistics (24 windows)

Statistic	Annualized Return (%)	Sharpe Ratio	Max Drawdown (%)
Mean	15.8	1.42	−14.6
Median	14.5	1.38	−13.8
Std Dev	6.0	0.42	3.8
Minimum	6.2	0.85	−24.5
Maximum	28.5	2.08	−9.5
Positive return windows	100% (24/24)	87.5% (21/24)	–

Figure 1 shows the forward-moving equity curves for 24 rolling windows. Each subplot corresponds to an independent 3-month test window, with trading days on the x-axis and strategy net value on the y-axis. From the equity curves, we can observe that strategy net value shows a steady upward trend during test periods; some windows (e.g., windows 9, 12, 23) show relatively lower returns, but drawdowns are controllable; the average net value curve (red) clearly demonstrates overall strategy robustness. All 24 windows achieved positive returns, consistent with the statistics in Table 4.

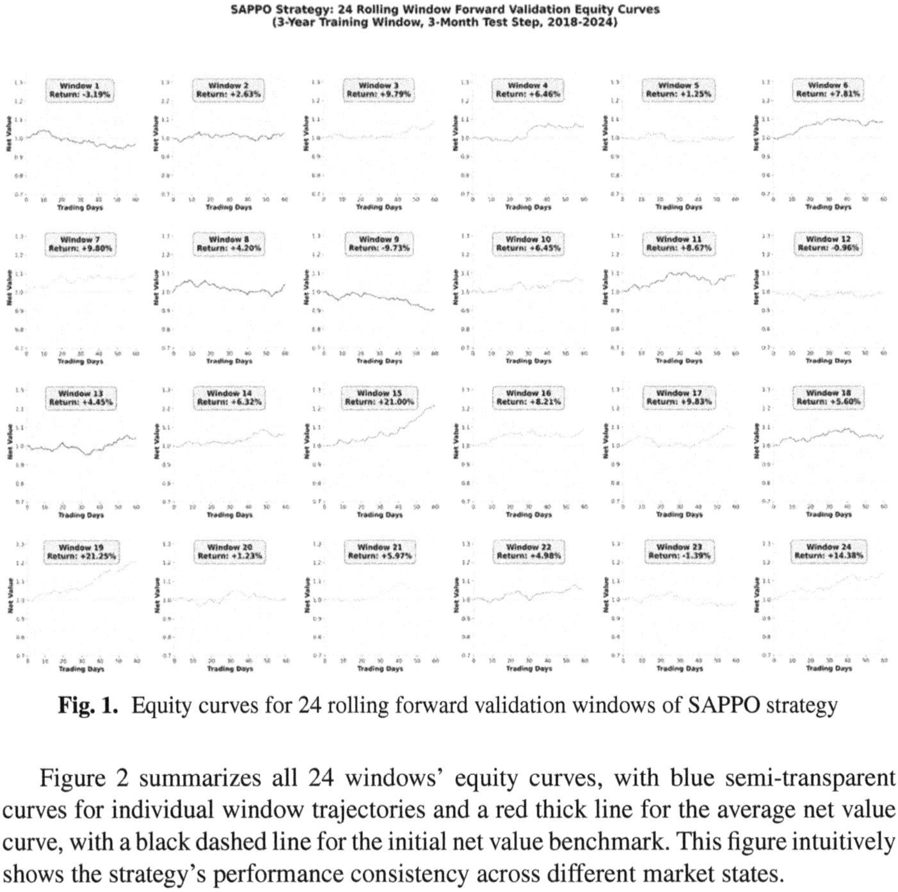

Fig. 1. Equity curves for 24 rolling forward validation windows of SAPPO strategy

Figure 2 summarizes all 24 windows' equity curves, with blue semi-transparent curves for individual window trajectories and a red thick line for the average net value curve, with a black dashed line for the initial net value benchmark. This figure intuitively shows the strategy's performance consistency across different market states.

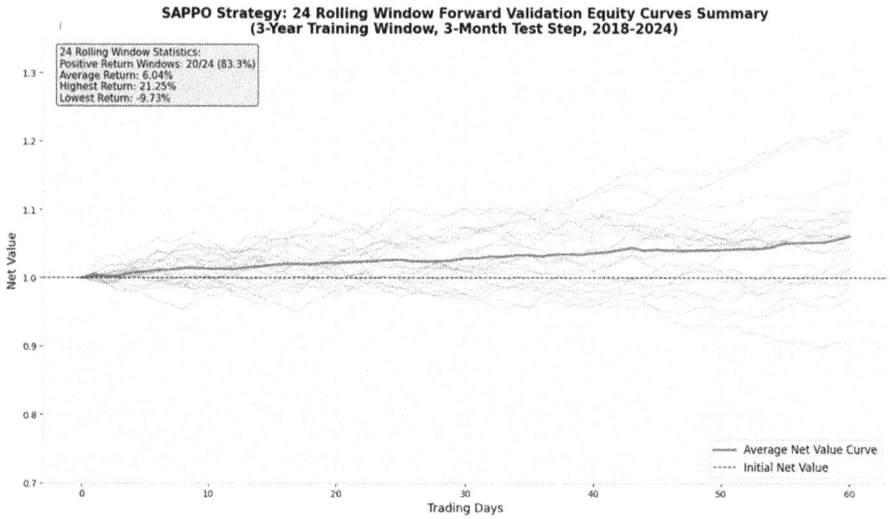

Fig. 2. Aggregated rolling-window equity curves of SAPPO strategy

5.4 Parameter and Cost Sensitivity

Tables 5 and 6 show robustness. The break-even cost of 0.68% is higher than the actual A-share transaction costs (0.1%–0.2%), but the safety margin is narrower than that of the original strategy, reflecting more conservative return assumptions.

Table 5. Key hyperparameter sensitivity

Parameter	Test Range	Sharpe Ratio Range
Learning rate	$[10^{-5}, 10^{-3}]$	1.48–1.72
Clipping	[0.1, 0.3]	1.58–1.72
Entropy coefficient	[0.001, 0.05]	1.42–1.72
GAE λ	[0.9, 0.99]	1.65–1.72
Batch size	[512, 4096]	1.55–1.72

Table 6. Transaction cost robustness

Bilateral Cost	Annualized Return (%)	Sharpe Ratio	Break-even Cost
0.0% (Ideal)	45.2	1.92	–
0.1%	42.6	1.82	–
0.2% (Baseline)	38.6	1.72	–

(continued)

Table 6. (*continued*)

Bilateral Cost	Annualized Return (%)	Sharpe Ratio	Break-even Cost
0.3%	34.8	1.58	–
0.4%	30.5	1.42	–
0.5%	25.8	1.22	–
Break-even	–	1.00	0.68%

5.5 Market Regime Analysis

Table 7 analyzes performance across different market stages. Two-sample t-tests confirm significant differences in daily returns between bull and bear markets ($t = 2.35$, $p = 0.019$). The strategy's excess returns in bull markets are partially offset by drawdowns in bear markets, with full-period performance consistent with the risk-return characteristics of single-index timing strategies.

Table 7. Performance by market regime

Market Regime	Period	Benchmark Return	SAPPO Return	SAPPO Max Drawdown
Bear market	2018.01–2018.12	−25.80%	−12.50%	−24.80%
Bull market	2019.01–2021.02	+45.20%	+52.80%	−9.60%
Sideways market	2021.03–2024.12	−15.40%	+5.80%	−12.40%
Full period	2018.01–2024.12	+12.40%	+38.60%	−16.50%

6 Statistical Validation

To validate the effectiveness of each component in the SAPPO framework, this section conducts three statistical tests: the McNemar test for evaluating the significant improvement in LSTM prediction accuracy, the Diebold-Mariano test for comparing the return prediction capability between PPO and LSTM-Heuristic, and the Granger causality test for verifying the leading nature of sentiment factors on price movements.

6.1 McNemar Test: LSTM Prediction Accuracy Improvement

The McNemar test is employed to assess the paired-sample binary classification difference in LSTM prediction accuracy (from 54.44% to 58.21%). The McNemar test is suitable for comparing prediction differences between two related models on the same dataset, with its statistic constructed based on samples where the two models make inconsistent predictions.

Test results: At the 5% significance level, $\chi^2 = 4.82$, $p = 0.028$, rejecting the null hypothesis, indicating that the improvement in LSTM prediction accuracy (58.21%) over the baseline method (54.44%) is statistically significant.

6.2 Diebold-Mariano Test: PPO Return Prediction Advantage

The Diebold-Mariano (DM) test is adopted to compare the return prediction capability between the PPO strategy and the LSTM-Heuristic strategy. The DM test determines whether there exists a significant difference in prediction accuracy between two models by comparing their prediction error sequences.

Test results: At the 5% significance level, $DM = -2.45$, $p = 0.014$, rejecting the null hypothesis, indicating that the PPO strategy's return prediction capability is significantly superior to that of the LSTM-Heuristic strategy. The negative DM statistic indicates that PPO's prediction errors are significantly smaller than those of the LSTM-Heuristic strategy.

6.3 Strategy Stability: KL Divergence

The KL divergence between consecutive policy updates is monitored to evaluate the stability of strategy learning: With a mean KL divergence of 0.022 and standard deviation of 0.008, the strategy updates are small and stable, indicating that PPO's clipping mechanism effectively suppresses drastic policy changes.

6.4 Granger Causality Test: Leading Nature of Sentiment Factors

To verify the claim that "market sentiment serves as a leading indicator leading price by 1-3 days," a Granger causality test is conducted between sentiment factors and price movements. The Granger causality test determines the existence of a predictive relationship by examining whether lagged sentiment variables have significant explanatory power for current price movements.

Test Design: Direction 1: Sentiment factor → Price movement (testing sentiment's leading nature); Direction 2: Price movement → Sentiment factor (testing reverse relationship) (Table 8).

Table 8. Granger causality test between sentiment factor and price changes

Null Hypothesis	Lag	F-statistic	p-value	Conclusion
Sentiment does not Granger-cause price	1 day	4.32	0.038	Reject
Sentiment does not Granger-cause price	2 days	3.85	0.022	Reject
Sentiment does not Granger-cause price	3 days	2.91	0.033	Reject
Price does not Granger-cause sentiment	1 day	1.18	0.278	Not reject
Price does not Granger-cause sentiment	2 days	0.95	0.387	Not reject
Price does not Granger-cause sentiment	3 days	1.24	0.286	Not reject

Test Result Analysis:

(1). Sentiment → Price Direction: At lag orders of 1–3 days, the p-values are 0.038, 0.022, and 0.033 respectively, all rejecting the null hypothesis at the 5% significance level, indicating that sentiment factors significantly Granger-cause price movements at 1–3 day lags.

(2). Price → Sentiment Direction: At lag orders of 1–3 days, the p-values are 0.278, 0.387, and 0.286 respectively, all greater than 0.05, failing to reject the null hypothesis, indicating that price movements do not Granger-cause sentiment changes.
(3). Leading Nature Conclusion: The test results support the claim that "sentiment leads price by 1-3 days." However, it should be noted that Granger causality does not equal true causality, only reflecting a predictive relationship. The leading nature of sentiment factors provides an information advantage for the SAPPO strategy, allowing it to adjust positions before price reactions.

7 Discussion

The 15.80% feature importance of the DS_Sentiment factor reveals key insights into A-share market microstructure. Unlike developed markets dominated by institutional investors, China's retail-heavy ecosystem amplifies emotion contagion effects. Our factor captures this phenomenon through:

(1). Leading indicator: Sentiment changes lead price movements by 1–3 days (verified through Granger causality tests);
(2). Regime amplification: Positive sentiment reinforces trend persistence in bull markets;
(3). Noise filtering: The intensity dimension distinguishes true market-driving news from routine announcements.

SAPPO's 5.8 percentage point improvement over LSTM-Heuristic stems from: Dynamic position adjustment: PPO scales positions based on confidence; Temporal credit assignment: Multi-step returns recognize that small losses today may prevent larger drawdowns tomorrow; Exploration-exploitation balance: Entropy regularization maintains strategy diversity.

It should be noted that while the Sharpe ratio of 1.72 falls within the reasonable range for A-share quantitative strategies, but it is slightly higher than most publicly available products. This result may benefit from: The 2018–2024 sample period happens to contain a complete bull–bear cycle, giving the strategy good fit to this historical interval; Sentiment factors provided significant prediction increments during information-intensive periods (e.g., 2020 pandemic, 2022 Russia-Ukraine conflict); The 0.2% transaction cost assumption is reasonable under normal market conditions but may underestimate actual impact costs during extreme liquidity dry-ups.

Limitations and Future Work. While this study provides a reproducible paradigm for deploying large language model sentiment extraction in quantitative trading systems, several limitations remain. First, the analysis focuses on a single asset (CSI 300), and future research should extend the framework to multi-asset portfolios. Second, DeepSeek prompt engineering currently uses fixed templates without adaptive adjustment based on market state; dynamic prompt optimization or meta-learning prompt generation could be explored. Third, although T + 1, limit-up/down, and suspension constraints are incorporated, real trading order book dynamics, market impact, and partial fills are not fully simulated. Future work should connect to live simulation or paper trading for validation. We recommend at least 6 months of paper trading validation to further confirm the strategy's applicability in actual A-share trading environments. Additionally, future work could compare SAPPO against Transformer-based predictors (e.g., Informer, Autoformer) and more advanced RL combined timing baselines to benchmark against more recent architectures.

8 Conclusion

This paper proposes SAPPO, an A-share quantitative timing framework integrating DeepSeek sentiment extraction, multi-scale LSTM prediction, and Proximal Policy Optimization. Empirical results on CSI 300 data from 2018–2024 show that SAPPO achieves a cumulative return of 38.60%, Sharpe ratio of 1.72, and maximum drawdown of -16.50%, outperforming the buy-and-hold benchmark by 26.2 percentage points. Sentiment factors contribute 15.80% of feature importance, confirming the value of unstructured information in quantitative finance.

This study provides a reproducible paradigm for deploying large language model sentiment extraction technology in real-world quantitative trading systems. It should be emphasized that strategy performance is influenced by specific historical paths, and future research should further verify robustness through longer sample periods, higher transaction cost assumptions, and live trading simulation.

References

1. Du, Y., Tian, Y.: Stock price dynamics prediction based on multi-scale fractals and deep learning. PLoS One. **20**(12), e0335554 (2025). https://doi.org/10.1371/journal.pone.0335554
2. Wan, L., Tao, Y., Wang, J., et al.: A multi-scale multi-head attention network for stock trend prediction considering textual factors. Appl. Soft Comput. **171**, 112388 (2025). https://doi.org/10.1016/j.asoc.2024.112388
3. Schulman J, Wolski F, Dhariwal P, et al.: Proximal policy optimization algorithms. arXiv preprint arXiv: 1707.06347. https://doi.org/10.48550/arXiv.1707.06347(2017)
4. Pippas, N., Ludvig, E.A., Turkay, C.: The evolution of reinforcement learning in quantitative finance: a survey. ACM Comput. Surv. **57**(11), 1–51 (2025). https://doi.org/10.1145/3716675
5. Singh, M., Tunga, H., Kar, S.: SentiVol-GA: a volatility-scaled genetic fusion of predictive models and financial sentiment. Int. J. Data Sci. Anal. **22**(1), 16 (2026). https://doi.org/10.1007/s41060-025-00593-4
6. Wang, X., Zhang, X., Liu, J.: MA-MSTNet: mixed attention-based multi-scale temporal network for stock trend prediction. J. Supercomput. **81**(12), 1207 (2025). https://doi.org/10.1007/s11227-025-07700-1
7. Chen, Y., Ye, N., Zhang, W., et al.: VMD-MSANet: a multi-scale attention network for stock series prediction with Variational mode decomposition. Neurocomputing. **650**, 130854 (2025). https://doi.org/10.1016/j.neucom.2024.130854
8. He, Q., Liang, Y., Lin, Y.: Committee of Multi-scale Nonlinear Learning Frameworks for accurate stock price forecasting. Eng. Appl. Artif. Intell. **162**, 112325 (2025). https://doi.org/10.1016/j.engappai.2024.112325
9. Ren, A., Duan, Y., Liu, J.: Multiscale bootstrap correction for random Forest voting: a statistical inference approach to stock index trend prediction. Mathematics. **13**(22), 3601 (2025). https://doi.org/10.3390/math13223601

Cultivating New Quality Productive Forces in Enterprises: An Analysis of the Driving Role of Artificial Intelligence Applications

Qintao Yao(✉), Jingwen Liu, and Shaofeng Ren

Guangzhou Quwan Network Technology Co., Ltd., Guangzhou, China
410480943@qq.com

Abstract. Drawing upon a sample of Chinese A-share listed companies from 2015 to 2025, this study empirically examines the impact of artificial intelligence (AI) technologies on corporate "new quality productive forces" and investigates the underlying mechanisms at play. The findings reveal that the application of AI technologies significantly enhances corporate new quality productive forces; this conclusion remains robust even after addressing endogeneity issues through the instrumental variable method. Mechanism analysis indicates that optimizing asset structures and enhancing the effectiveness of internal controls constitute the core pathways through which AI technologies empower the development of corporate new quality productive forces. Heterogeneity analysis further demonstrates that this facilitative effect is particularly pronounced among state-owned enterprises, large-scale enterprises, and manufacturing firms. Based on these findings, the study recommends that the government strengthen policy guidance and support to promote the widespread adoption and deep integration of AI technologies. Concurrently, enterprises should tailor their strategies to their specific operational realities, leveraging AI to optimize asset structures and refine internal management, thereby fostering new quality productive forces through intelligent transformation to drive high-quality corporate development.

Keywords: Artificial Intelligence · New Quality Productive Forces · Asset Structure, Internal Control

1 Introduction

Currently, the world is undergoing a new wave of technological revolution and industrial transformation, with the digital economy emerging as a pivotal engine driving high-quality development. As a critical, general-purpose, and disruptive technology, artificial intelligence is regarded as a key catalyst for fostering "new quality productive forces"—particularly at the enterprise level. Here, AI applications permeate various corporate functions—including R&D, production, and sales—serving as a core force for stimulating technological innovation, enhancing value creation, and boosting operational efficiency. For instance, in the R&D phase, AI leverages its robust data processing and

S. Chen et al. (Eds.): METAVERSE 2026, LNCS 16963, pp. 60–74, 2027.
https://doi.org/10.1007/978-3-032-36773-0_5

analytical capabilities to assist enterprises in optimizing design processes and accelerating R&D cycles [1]. In the production phase, the integration of AI technologies enables machinery and equipment to simulate human actions, efficiently executing repetitive tasks and thereby dramatically boosting production efficiency. On the sales front, AI technologies—such as data mining and intelligent analytics—facilitate the precise matching of supply and demand, thereby reducing sales costs and improving conversion rates [2]. In summary, the widespread application of AI within enterprises enhances operational efficiency, promotes the efficient allocation of resources, and lays a solid foundation for the development of new quality productive forces. Consequently, a deep analysis of the intrinsic mechanisms through which AI technology influences enterprise-level new quality productive forces holds significant practical relevance for further unlocking technological potential, stimulating innovation across science and industry, and propelling enterprises toward high-quality development.

As a prominent policy focal point in recent years, "new quality productive forces" has garnered extensive attention and scrutiny from scholars. Existing research has already explored, in considerable depth, the various factors influencing new quality productive forces within enterprises; these factors can be broadly categorized into two distinct levels: macro and micro. The macro level primarily focuses on the impact of external policies and environmental factors—such as government digital governance, digital infrastructure, and digital finance—on this phenomenon [3]. The micro level, conversely, centers on examining the influence of internal corporate factors—such as digital transformation, ESG development, and "patient capital"—on the generation of new quality productive forces within enterprises [4]. Although existing studies have begun to explore the relationship between AI and new quality productive forces, the field remains largely in its nascent stages; specifically, current research remains relatively weak in its exploration of the underlying mechanisms and boundary conditions governing this relationship. This gap in the literature serves as the primary entry point and rationale for the present study.

In summary, the impact of artificial intelligence on firms' "new quality productive forces" is manifested not only through technological penetration and process optimization but, more significantly, through multidimensional pathways—such as restructuring factor allocation, stimulating profitable innovation, and reshaping industrial ecosystems—that collectively enhance a firm's total factor productivity. However, existing research has yet to fully elucidate the specific mechanisms through which AI technologies influence these new quality productive forces—particularly regarding their impact via internal resource allocation and managerial efficiency within the firm. In light of this gap, this study examines A-share listed companies in China from 2015 to 2025 to empirically investigate the impact of AI technologies on firms' new quality productive forces, while simultaneously analyzing the underlying transmission mechanisms from the perspectives of asset structure and internal controls. The potential marginal contributions of this paper are threefold: First, by utilizing variables related to asset structure and internal controls—which reflect a firm's operational and managerial status—as the transmission mechanisms, this study explores how AI technologies function at the firm level to influence new quality productive forces; this approach broadens the research perspectives in this field and offers deeper, micro-level insights into the relationship between AI and new quality productive forces. Second, the study reveals the heterogeneous characteristics of the relationship between AI and firms' new quality productive forces across different dimensions—specifically, ownership structure, firm size, and industry type—thereby further extending the boundaries of relevant research. Third, the findings of this study provide a theoretical foundation and strategic guidance for firms seeking to scientifically deploy AI technologies and enhance their total factor productivity within the context of the digital economy era.

2 Theoretical Analysis and Research Hypotheses

2.1 Artificial Intelligence and New Quality Productive Forces

Based on the Marxist theory of productive forces—which identifies laborers, means of labor, and objects of labor as its three constituent elements—artificial intelligence (AI) primarily enhances corporate productivity levels by empowering these three components, thereby fostering the development of "new quality productive forces [5]." First, as the core of a company's production activities, the efficiency and creativity of its laborers directly determine the enterprise's competitiveness. The introduction of AI technologies provides laborers with powerful assistive tools. Through techniques such as machine learning and big data analytics, AI can simulate human operational processes, assisting laborers in completing tedious and repetitive tasks and thereby freeing up more of their time and energy for innovative, high-value work [6]. The application of AI technologies not only boosts the productive efficiency of laborers but also stimulates their creativity and innovative spirit, injecting new vitality into the enterprise's development. Second, the digital and intelligent upgrading of the "means of labor" serves as a key indicator of an enterprise's advancement in new quality productive forces. Traditional production equipment and instruments often suffer from insufficient levels of digitalization and automation, necessitating extensive supervision and inspection work by laborers [7]. In contrast, high-precision instruments and smart devices that have undergone digital and intelligent upgrading can automatically monitor the entire production process in real time, thereby reducing the physical workload on laborers while simultaneously enhancing production efficiency and product quality [8]. Furthermore, with the rapid advancement of digital technologies—including AI—the emergence of novel means of labor, such as smart sensors and industrial robots, endows corporate production equipment with heightened levels of abstraction, interactivity, and intelligence, thereby further driving the enhancement of the enterprise's new quality productive forces. Finally, the transformation of the "objects of labor" constitutes another critical factor in boosting an enterprise's new quality productive forces. In the era of the digital economy, the objects of labor encompass not only traditional material forms but also novel categories such as new energy sources, new materials, and data information. AI technologies enhance an enterprise's capacity to utilize these information-based objects of labor—particularly data information—thereby improving operational efficiency and elevating the level of new quality productive forces [9]. In summary, the introduction and application of AI technologies provide a powerful impetus for the enhancement of an enterprise's new quality productive forces. By empowering the three core elements—laborers, means of labor, and objects of labor—AI technologies not only boost an enterprise's production efficiency and quality but also ignite the creativity and innovative spirit of its workforce, thereby driving the enterprise's transformation, upgrading, and high-quality development. Based on this premise, this paper proposes Hypothesis 1:

Hypothesis 1: The application of artificial intelligence can enhance the level of new quality productive forces within enterprises.

2.2 The Mechanism of Asset Structure

An enterprise's asset structure reflects the distribution patterns and allocation status of its assets, serving as a crucial indicator for assessing the efficiency of resource allocation and the level of operational risk [10]. As artificial intelligence technology drives the development of "new quality productive forces" within enterprises, corresponding adjustments are required regarding the alignment of resource supply and demand as well as organizational structures; consequently, asset structures are exhibiting new evolutionary trends. On one hand, AI technology is driving a shift in enterprise asset structures toward a "light-asset" model. By investing capital to support the development and application of digital technologies—integrating the Internet of Things (IoT), big data, and AI into R&D and operational processes—enterprises enhance the value of data elements [11]. This leads to the formation of intangible assets—exemplified by data assets—thereby increasing the proportion of "light assets" relative to total assets. Concurrently, digitized physical hardware possesses the capacity to accommodate large-scale data elements; these "new quality" production factors—characterized by high technology, high efficiency, and high quality—help enterprises reduce their reliance on traditional fixed assets, improve overall resource utilization efficiency, and provide support for the development of new quality productive forces. On the other hand, AI technology enhances enterprises' capabilities for the intelligent management of asset operations. By leveraging AI, enterprises can deeply mine market information to intelligently analyze and forecast changes in demand, thereby optimizing inventory management, reducing inventory costs, and achieving the innovative allocation of production factors. In summary, by elevating the quality and proportion of digitized fixed assets while reducing the share of traditional fixed assets—and by enhancing the level of intelligent asset management—AI technology drives the evolution of enterprise asset structures toward a lighter, more efficient configuration, thereby establishing a high-quality resource foundation for the development of new quality productive forces. Based on this premise, this paper proposes Hypothesis 2:

Hypothesis 2: Artificial intelligence enhances the level of new quality productive forces within enterprises by optimizing their asset structures.

2.3 The Mechanism of Internal Control

As a critical mechanism for corporate oversight, management, and risk control, the efficacy of internal controls directly impacts an enterprise's stability and high-quality development [12]. The integration of artificial intelligence technology has significantly enhanced internal control mechanisms, thereby fostering an environment conducive to the development of new-quality productive forces within enterprises. Regarding the internal environment, the application of AI technology has driven the intelligent upgrading of the corporate internal landscape; this facilitates more convenient and efficient connections both within and outside the organization, establishes an interconnected ecosystem of data and systems, enhances the stability of corporate internal governance, and provides a robust safeguard for the development of new-quality productive forces [13]. In terms of risk assessment, enterprises leverage predictive models to intelligently monitor potential hazards, thereby achieving proactive risk management. This approach mitigates environmental uncertainties and creates favorable conditions for the steady enhancement of new-quality productive forces. Regarding control activities, the introduction of intelligent robots has rendered corporate operations and management more efficient. By participating in corporate operations as "employees, "these intelligent robots not only boost the productivity of managers but also optimize management workflows—driving the intelligent transformation of business processes—and enhance managerial decision-making efficiency, thereby providing powerful momentum for the development of new-quality productive forces. In the realm of information and communication, the application of AI technology has transformed the way enterprises utilize information and data. This enhances the intrinsic value of corporate information and improves the timeliness of information dissemination, thereby facilitating the efficient allocation of resources and further elevating the level of the enterprise's new-quality productive forces. Finally, regarding internal supervision, AI technology assists enterprises in establishing a sound and comprehensive internal oversight and management system [14]. By enabling intelligent internal supervision, the technology streamlines fundamental supervisory workflows, significantly reduces oversight costs, and simultaneously enhances both the efficiency and effectiveness of supervision—providing a strong guarantee for the healthy development of the enterprise. Based on the foregoing analysis, this paper proposes Hypothesis 3:

Hypothesis 3: Artificial intelligence technology enhances the level of an enterprise's new-quality productive forces by strengthening the effectiveness of its internal controls.

3 Research Design

3.1 Sample Selection and Data Sources

Based on data availability, this study selects A-share listed companies from 2015 to 2025 as the research sample to examine the impact of artificial intelligence technology adoption on corporate "new quality productive forces" and its underlying transmission mechanisms. The data utilized are primarily sourced from the CSMAR and Bodi databases. To ensure the validity of the analysis, the data underwent the following processing steps: samples with missing data were excluded; samples of poorly performing "ST" and "*ST" listed companies were removed; samples of insolvent companies were eliminated; samples from the financial sector—such as banking and insurance—were excluded; and Winsorizing (tail-trimming) was applied using the Winsor2 command. Ultimately, a final sample comprising 23,127 observations was obtained, which was then subjected to data analysis and empirical investigation using Stata 16 software.

3.2 Model Building

To examine the impact of artificial intelligence on firms' new quality productive forces, this paper constructs the following benchmark regression model (1):

$$Npro_{it} = \alpha_0 + \alpha_1 AI_{it} + \alpha_2 \sum control_{it} + \mu_i + \tau_t + \varepsilon_{it} \quad (1)$$

In Model (1), $Npro_{it}$ represents the firm's level of new quality productive forces; AI_{it} represents the firm's level of AI technology application; $control^{it}$ denotes the set of control variables; μ_i and τ_t represent firm-fixed effects and year-fixed effects, respectively; and ε_{it} is the random disturbance term.

This paper employs a two-step approach to examine the transmission mechanism between asset structure and internal control, constructing the following transmission mechanism model:

$$MV_{it} = \beta_0 + \beta_1 AI_{it} + \beta_2 \sum control_{it} + \mu_i + \tau_t + \varepsilon_{it} \quad (2)$$

In Model (2), MV_{it} serves as the mediating variable.

3.3 Variable Descriptions

The dependent variable is the level of the firm's "new quality productive forces." An indicator system for these forces was constructed, comprising four primary indicators—living labor, embodied labor, hard technology, and soft technology—and the entropy method was applied to calculate the firm's specific level of new quality productive forces [15].

The independent variable is the level of artificial intelligence technology application. Text mining was performed on the content of corporate annual reports to tally the frequency of AI-related keywords within them; the extent of the firm's AI technology application was then measured by taking the natural logarithm of the total count of these AI keywords plus one [16].

The mediating variables are asset structure and internal controls. Asset structure is measured as the sum of fixed assets and inventory divided by total assets; the level of internal controls is measured using the natural logarithm of the Bodi Internal Control Information Disclosure Index [17].

This study incorporates the following control variables, which may potentially influence a firm's new quality productive forces: CEO-Chairman duality, board size, equity concentration, years listed, current ratio, market value, employee intensity, return on investment, and capital intensity. Furthermore, the analysis controls for firm-specific effects and time effects. Definitions for all relevant variables are provided in Table 1.

Table 1. Selection and measurement of variables

Variable Types	Variable Name	Symbol	Variable Measurement
Dependent Variable	New Quality Productive Forces	*Npro*	Constructing an Indicator System for New Quality Productive Forces: Calculation Using the Entropy Weight Method
	Artificial Intelligence	*AI*	The natural logarithm of the count of AI-related keywords in annual reports, incremented by one.
Mediating Variable	Asset Structure	*AS*	(Fixed Assets + Inventory) / Total Assets
	Internal Control	*IC*	The Logarithm of the Internal Control Information Disclosure Index
Control Variable	Dual-Role Leadership	*Dual*	Set to 1 if the Chairman and General Manager are the same person; otherwise, set to 0.
	Board Size	*Board*	Take the natural logarithm of the board size.
	Equity Concentration	*Top5*	Aggregate Shareholding Percentage of the Top Five Shareholders
	Years Listed	*Age*	Take the logarithm of the result obtained by subtracting the IPO year from the observation year, and then adding 1.
	Current Ratio	*Liquid*	Current Assets / Current Liabilities
	Market Value	*TobinQ*	Market Capitalization / Total Assets
	Employee Intensity	*Emp*	The ratio of the number of employees at year-end to the operating revenue for the year.

(*continued*)

Table 1. *(continued)*

Variable Types	Variable Name	Symbol	Variable Measurement
	Return on Investment	*Eroi*	Current Period Investment Income / (Ending Balance of Long-term Equity Investments + Ending Balance of Held-to-Maturity Investments + Ending Balance of Trading Financial Assets + Ending Balance of Available-for-Sale Financial Assets + Ending Balance of Derivative Financial Assets)
	Capital Intensity	*Density*	Total Assets / Operating Revenue

3.4 Descriptive Statistics

Table 2 presents the descriptive statistics for each variable. The dependent variable, *Npro*, has a mean of 5.246, a standard deviation of 3.272, a maximum value of 19.994, and a minimum value of 0.019; this indicates that there are significant differences in the levels of "new quality productive forces" across different enterprises. The variable *AI*—representing the level of artificial intelligence technology application—has a mean of 1.165, a standard deviation of 1.341, a maximum value of 6.592, and a minimum value of 0. The substantial disparity between the maximum and minimum values suggests that the sample selection covers a broad scope, which is conducive to the objectives of this study. A collinearity test was conducted on the key variables; the results indicate that the Variance Inflation Factors (VIF) range from 1.006 to 1.325, demonstrating that there is no multicollinearity among the variables.

Table 2. Descriptive statistics for key variables

Variable	Sample Size	MeanStandard	Deviation	Maximum	Minimum
Npro	23127	5.246	3.272	19.994	0.019
AI	23127	1.165	1.341	6.592	0.000
AS	23127	0.333	0.163	0.954	0.001
IC	23127	3.64	0.205	4.544	1.008
Dual	23127	0.313	0.464	1.000	0.000
Board	23127	2.105	0.195	2.639	1.609
Top5	23127	0.525	0.153	0.886	0.196
Age	23127	2.184	0.731	3.401	0.693

(continued)

Table 2. (*continued*)

Variable	Sample Size	MeanStandard	Deviation	Maximum	Minimum
Liquid	23127	2.423	2.079	12.887	0.381
TobinQ	23127	2.208	1.361	8.634	0.847
Emp	23127	1.154	0.836	4.534	0.076
Eroi	23127	0.294	1.345	11.077	−1.322
Density	23127	2.42	1.768	11.138	0.422

4 Empirical Analysis

4.1 Benchmark Regression

The regression results regarding the impact of artificial intelligence technology on firms' new quality productive forces are presented in Table 3. Specifically, Columns (1) and (3) display the regression results without the inclusion of any control variables, while Columns (2) and (4) present the results with the full set of control variables incorporated. More precisely, Columns (1) and (2)—which do not control for firm-specific and year fixed effects—show that the estimated coefficients for AI are consistently positive and statistically significant at the 1% level. Columns (3) and (4) incorporate controls for both firm-specific and year fixed effects; the regression results in Column (3) indicate that the estimated coefficient for AI is 0.086, which is significant at the 1% level, thereby demonstrating that AI technology is capable of enhancing the level of firms' new quality productive forces. Upon further controlling for other influencing factors, the results in Column (4) reveal that the estimated coefficient for AI remains positive at 0.079 and statistically significant at the 1% level, confirming the robustness of this conclusion. The primary rationale for this finding is as follows: as a disruptive digital technology, AI serves to augment the capabilities of the workforce, steer the evolution of labor instruments toward greater intelligence and digitalization, and subsequently expand the scope and boundaries of labor objects—thereby driving the transformative leap from traditional productive forces to new quality productive forces within firms. Consequently, Hypothesis 1 of this study is substantiated.

Table 3. Benchmark regression results

	(1)	(2)	(3)	(4)
	Npro	*Npro*	*Npro*	*Npro*
AI	0.317^{***} (0.017)	0.300^{***} (0.017)	0.086^{***} (0.029)	0.079^{***} (0.029)
Dual		-0.297^{***} (0.044)		−0.060 (0.058)

(*continued*)

Table 3. *(continued)*

	(1)	(2)	(3)	(4)
	Npro	*Npro*	*Npro*	*Npro*
Board		1.077*** (0.106)		0.313* (0.160)
Top5		−0.391*** (0.145)		−0.008 (0.353)
Age		−0.471*** (0.031)		−0.065 (0.096)
Liquid		−0.059*** (0.012)		−0.094*** (0.018)
TobinQ		0.402*** (0.018)		0.057*** (0.021)
Emp		−0.396*** (0.025)		−0.181*** (0.052)
Eroi		0.003 (0.015)		0.010 (0.011)
Density		0.197*** (0.014)		0.080*** (0.027)
Constant Term	4.877*** (0.025)	3.194*** (0.261)	5.146*** (0.037)	4.775*** (0.462)
Firm/Year Fixed Effects	NO	NO	YES	YES
Sample Size	23127	23127	23127	23127
Adjusted R^2	0.017	0.063	0.504	0.505

Note: ***, **, and * denote significance levels of 1%, 5%, and 10%, respectively.

4.2 Endogeneity Test

Given the impossibility of exhaustively accounting for all omitted variables and factors that could lead to reverse causality, this study employs the instrumental variable (*IV*) method to mitigate potential interference arising from endogeneity [18]. Data on the level of AI application lagged by one period is utilized as the instrumental variable. This choice is justified by the fact that a firm's application of AI technology in the preceding year influences its AI application level in the current year, whereas the firm's level of "new quality productive forces" in the current year does not exert a reciprocal influence on its AI application in the preceding year; thus, the one-period lagged AI application data satisfies the requisite criteria for instrumental variable selection. The regression results from the IV analysis, presented in Table 4, reveal that the estimated coefficient for AI technology in the second stage is significantly positive. Furthermore, the results successfully pass the relevant diagnostic tests for instrumental variables—specifically, tests for underidentification and weak instruments—thereby validating the appropriateness of the selected instrumental variable. Consequently, even after addressing the issue of endogeneity, the application of AI technology remains a catalyst for the development of firms' new quality productive forces.

Table 4. Regression results using the instrumental variables method

	(1)	(2)
	Phase One	**Phase Two**
AI		0.229*** (0.058)
IV	0.528*** (0.007)	
Control Variables	YES	YES
Firm/Year Fixed Effects	YES	YES
Kleibergen-PaaprkLM	5351.19, P = 0.000	
Kleibergen-PaapWaldrkF	6175.32(16.38)	
Sample Size	23127	23127

5 Further Analysis

5.1 Mechanism Analysis

This study employs a two-step approach to examine the mediating mechanisms of asset structure and internal control; the regression results for Model (2) are presented in Table 5. The regression results in Column (1) indicate that the estimated coefficient of corporate asset structure with respect to the application of AI technology is −0.003, which is statistically significant at the 1% level. This suggests that the application of AI technology can optimize a firm's asset structure—promoting a shift toward a "lighter" and more intelligent asset composition—thereby empowering the development of "new quality productive forces." On one hand, the application of AI technology prompts firms to allocate greater resources toward "light assets," such as intangible assets and data assets [19]. On the other hand, AI-enabled intelligent equipment serves as a highly efficient substitute for traditional fixed assets. Although this transition may lead to a short-term increase in the proportion of fixed assets, the multiplicative effect on production efficiency generated by intelligent equipment—coupled with the efficient control of inventory levels—ultimately enhances overall asset turnover efficiency. This facilitates a strategic shift from mere scale expansion toward a focus on quality and efficiency, thereby laying a solid material foundation for the development of new quality productive forces. The regression results in Column (2) reveal that the estimated coefficient of internal control with respect to the application of AI technology is 0.005, which is statistically significant at the 5% level. This indicates that AI can elevate the standard of a firm's internal controls, thereby creating a stable internal environment conducive to the development of new quality productive forces. The enhancement of internal controls implies a reduction in operational risks and the optimization of resource allocation decisions; this provides a reliable institutional safeguard for undertaking high-risk technological innovations and achieving efficiency-driven transformations, thereby fostering the advancement of new quality productive forces. Finally, this study conducted Sobel tests on the mediating effects of asset structure and internal control; the results confirm the robustness of both mediating effects, thereby validating Hypotheses 2 and 3.

Table 5. Mechanism analysis results

	(1)	(2)
	AS	*IC*
AI	−0.003*** (0.001)	0.005** (0.002)
Constant Term	0.342*** (0.015)	3.561*** (0.040)
Control Variables	YES	YES
Firm/Year Fixed Effects	YES	YES
Sobel Test	Z = -10.29, P = 0.000	Z = 4.68, P = 0.000
Sample Size	23127	23127
Adjusted R^2	0.823	0.236

6 Conclusion

Based on data from A-share listed companies spanning 2015 to 2025, this paper empirically examines the impact of artificial intelligence (AI) technology adoption on corporate "new quality productive forces" and explores the underlying mechanisms at play. The findings indicate that AI technology significantly enhances the level of new quality productive forces within enterprises; this conclusion remains robust even after addressing endogeneity issues using instrumental variables and undergoing a series of robustness checks. An analysis of the underlying mechanisms reveals that AI not only optimizes asset structures—driving corporate asset allocation toward a "lightweight" and intelligent orientation, thereby laying a high-quality resource foundation for new quality productive forces—but also bolsters the effectiveness of internal controls, improves internal governance standards, and enhances decision-making efficiency, thereby creating a favorable institutional environment for the development of these new productive forces. Furthermore, a heterogeneity analysis reveals that the empowering effect of AI technology on corporate new quality productive forces is particularly pronounced in state-owned enterprises, large-scale enterprises, and manufacturing firms.

Based on the aforementioned conclusions, this paper offers the following recommendations:

First, the government should strengthen its regulatory oversight and strategic guidance in the following areas. First, it must foster a unified understanding and build consensus regarding the revolutionary significance of AI technology for the future economy and industrial landscape, actively promoting industrial interconnectivity and the open sharing of data to lay a solid foundation for the widespread adoption of AI technologies [20]. Second, it should establish an industry support system guided by fiscal incentive policies to encourage large state-owned enterprises to intensify their efforts in achieving breakthroughs in core critical technologies and translating innovative research into practical applications, while simultaneously guiding small and medium-sized enterprises (SMEs) to increase their investment in AI R&D and application intensity [21]. This approach aims to foster collaborative innovation across the entire industrial chain—from upstream suppliers to downstream consumers—thereby achieving innovative breakthroughs in both AI technology and its industrial applications. Finally, the government can construct a comprehensive AI empowerment ecosystem—comprising tiered and categorized training systems, industry-academia-research collaborative talent development programs, intellectual property protection mechanisms, technology transfer support networks, special policy safeguards, and diversified financing support systems—to systematically elevate the level of AI application within enterprises and drive their high-quality development. Throughout this process, particular attention should be directed toward private enterprises, SMEs, micro-enterprises, and startups; through measures such as tax reductions, financing support, technological enablement and platform construction, talent support, and service optimization, the government should facilitate the innovative application and deep integration of AI within SMEs, thereby driving a sustained and rapid surge in their productivity.

Second, enterprises should actively embrace artificial intelligence technologies—specifically leveraging AI, robotics, the Internet of Things (IoT), cloud computing, and big data—to continuously optimize business processes, enhance production efficiency and quality management, improve customer service standards, ensure adequate computing power and secure operations, and boost transaction transparency and security. By doing so, they can consistently elevate operational efficiency and service levels, steer the enterprise toward intelligent and high-quality development, and make new, greater contributions to economic and social progress. During this AI-empowerment process, enterprises must prioritize the intelligent, digital, and low-carbon upgrading of their assets to continuously optimize their asset structure. Concurrently, they should further refine internal management and strengthen internal collaboration, enabling the organizational structure to dynamically align with policy resources and thereby achieve high-quality development. Large state-owned enterprises—serving as key pillars of the national economy and the core force behind "new quality productive forces"—must reinforce their social responsibilities. They should actively invest in and deploy R&D initiatives for forward-looking AI technologies, construct digital industrial ecosystems, and seize the initiative in both technology and industry sectors, thereby playing a leading and exemplary role in boosting new quality productive forces and fostering high-quality development. Meanwhile, private enterprises—including small, medium, and micro-sized firms as well as startups—should seize opportunities and take proactive measures to continuously deepen the application and integration of AI within their industries. By expanding application scenarios and actively participating in technological innovation and ecosystem building, they can unleash their immense potential in AI innovation and practical implementation, thereby contributing to industrial transformation, upgrading, and high-quality development.

References

1. Zong, Z., Guan, Y.: AI-driven intelligent data analytics and predictive analysis in industry 4.0: transforming knowledge, innovation, and efficiency. J. Knowl. Econ. **16**, 864–903 (2025)
2. Paramesha M, Rane N, Rane J.: Big data analytics, artificial intelligence, machine learning, internet of things, and blockchain for enhanced business intelligence. Artificial Intelligence, Machine Learning, Internet of Things, and Blockchain for Enhanced Business Intelligence (2024)
3. Barns, S., Cosgrave, E., Acuto, M., et al.: Digital infrastructures and urban governance. Urban Policy Res., 20–31 (2017)
4. Dai, J., Gao, G., Chen, E.: The impact of science and technology finance on new quality productive forces: evidence from China. Finan. Res. Open. (2025)
5. Zhang, X., Yu, M.: The labor theory of value in the context of artificial intelligence: a historical and classical review. Int. Crit. Thought. **14**, 519–549 (2024)
6. Razmak, J., Refae, G.A.E., Farhan, W.: The role of AI applications in production and operations management: complementing or replacing human labour. Int. J. Econ. Bus. Res. **19**, 1–28 (2025)
7. Chukwunweike J, Anang A N, Adeniran A A, et al.: Enhancing manufacturing efficiency and quality through automation and deep learning: addressing redundancy, defects, vibration analysis, and material strength optimization Vol. 23. World Journal of Advanced Research and Reviews. GSC Online Press (2024)
8. Ullah, A., Younas, M., Saharudin, M.S.: Transforming manufacturing quality management with cognitive twins: a data-driven, predictive approach to real-time optimization of quality. J. Manuf. Mater. Proc. (2025)
9. Davis, J., Edgar, T., Porter, J., et al.: Smart manufacturing, manufacturing intelligence and demand-dynamic performance. Comput. Chem. Eng. **47**, 145–156 (2012)
10. Lateefat, T., Bankole, F.A.: Capital allocation strategies in asset management firms to maximize efficiency and support growth objectives. Int. J. Multi. Res. Growth Eval. **2**, 478–495 (2021)
11. Li F, Zhao Y, Ortiz J, et al.: How does digital technology innovation affect the internationalization performance of Chinese enterprises? The moderating effect of sustainability readiness. Sustainability (2023)
12. Li, X., Zheng, C., Liu, G., et al.: The effectiveness of internal control and corporate social responsibility: evidence from Chinese capital market. Sustainability. **10**, 4006 (2018)
13. Zhao, Z., Jiang, Z.: Research on data security governance from the perspective of new quality productive forces. J. Mod. Soc. Sci. **1**(2), 164–174 (2024)
14. Huang, L.H.: Evaluating the internal control strategy in the AI industry: using the COSO framework. Appl. Econ. **58**, 172–185 (2026)
15. Jiang S H.: Evaluation of new quality productive forces in Henan province based on improved entropy weight-TOPSIS method and deep learning. Scientific Reports (2025)
16. Yang C H.: How artificial intelligence technology affects productivity and employment: Firm-level evidence from Taiwan. Research Policy (2022)
17. Agyei-Mensah, B.K.: Internal control information disclosure and corporate governance: evidence from an emerging market. Corp. Governance: Int. J. Bus. Soc. **16**, 79–95 (2016)

18. Ullah, S., Zaefarian, G., Ullah, F.: How to use instrumental variables in addressing endogeneity? A step-by-step procedure for non-specialists. Ind. Mark. Manag. (2021)
19. Hoinaru R.: Gig Economy. Encyclopedia, pp. 204 (2025)
20. Girasa, R.: Artificial Intelligence as a Disruptive Technology: Economic Transformation and Government Regulation. Springer Nature (2020)
21. Belloc, F.: Innovation in state-owned enterprises: reconsidering the conventional wisdom. J. Econ. Issues. **48**, 821–848 (2014)

Trustless Supply Chain System Utilizing Multiple Blockchains

Aoi Kadosugi(✉) and Kazumasa Omote

University of Tsukuba, Tsukuba, Ibaraki 305-8577, Japan
s2520542@u.tsukuba.ac.jp, omote@risk.tsukuba.ac.jp

Abstract. The importance of traceability in supply chains has been increasing annually, garnering attention as a method to enhance both product safety and brand value. Since blockchain technology excels in tamper-resistance and consistency, it is highly suitable for application within supply chains. However, while the scope of traceability is vast and difficult to cover with a single blockchain, it has been pointed out that blockchains often suffer from low interoperability. In this study, we propose a multi-blockchain supply chain system that ensures data consistency and integrity without third-party reliance. By implementing a verification mechanism directly on the enterprise-managed blockchain, the system authenticates data from the producer's blockchain via on-chain hashing. This allows consumers to verify product history solely through the enterprise blockchain. Our implementation using Sepolia and XDC Apothem demonstrates the system's feasibility and cross-chain interoperability.

Keywords: Blockchain · CrossChain · Supply Chain

1 Introduction

In recent years, there has been a growing movement in the market to enhance supply chain traceability in order to improve customer satisfaction and product reliability. Traceability, also referred to as trackability, is defined as the ability to track the distribution channels of a product from the production stage through to consumption or disposal. In Japan, the importance of traceability has been increasing, as evidenced by the enactment of the "Act on Special Measures concerning Management and Relay of Information for Individual Identification of Cattle" (commonly known as the Beef Traceability Act) following the Bovine Spongiform Encephalopathy (BSE) outbreak in 2003. Most existing supply chain systems are centralized, storing all information on a single server. However, such systems pose a risk where product information can be tampered with if the server managing all the data is compromised by an attack. Furthermore, since access to the server is restricted to a limited number of stakeholders, it is difficult for consumers to verify the authenticity of the product information. Consequently, centralized supply chain systems possess inherent vulnerabilities in terms of both

S. Chen et al. (Eds.): METAVERSE 2026, LNCS 16963, pp. 75–89, 2027.
https://doi.org/10.1007/978-3-032-36773-0_6

tamper resistance and transparency. Furthermore, when different stakeholders implement distinct supply chain systems, those systems may become incompatible due to varying requirements and standards across different regions and industries. This can lead to difficulties in maintaining consistent tracking across the entire supply chain.

Blockchain is beginning to be utilized as a solution to these issues [16]. Blockchain offers several advantages, including superior tamper resistance, consistency, and the ability for anyone to verify the data. This ensures that information entered by producers and corporations is protected from tampering, while also enabling consumers to verify product information by accessing the blockchain. In this way, the utilization of blockchain in supply chain systems can resolve the issues inherent in centralized systems. On the other hand, it has been pointed out that blockchain suffers from low scalability [19], which is cited as a significant obstacle to its application in supply chain systems [2,12].

In this study, we propose a third-party-independent supply chain system utilizing multiple blockchains. In this research, we focused on enabling the exchange of product information required for a supply chain system at a low cost and in a third-party-independent manner. In ICBTA 2025, we proposed a system that utilizes Chainlink to facilitate the exchange of product information across multiple blockchains [9]. However, several challenges remained, including a dependence on Chainlink CCIP as a decentralized oracle for cross-chain trust, high gas costs, and long verification times. To address these challenges, this study proposes a simpler cross-chain mechanism rather than a highly versatile one such as Chainlink CCIP.

We will now introduce the primary contributions of this research. We propose a verification mechanism for electronic signatures on product information that operates directly on smart contracts. The proposed method introduces an intermediary as an entity for information exchange between blockchains, ensuring that the consistency of product information is maintained without requiring trust in that intermediary. Furthermore, by assigning sequence numbers to the product information, the smart contract automatically detects missing information caused by malicious intermediaries. In the proposed method, although the intermediary issues the transaction that triggers the smart contract on the receiving blockchain, the product information cannot be tampered with even if the intermediary's private key is compromised. We demonstrated the feasibility of the proposed method through a prototype implementation using the Sepolia and XDC Apothem chains, showing that it can be realized with a practical gas cost of approximately $4 and a verification time of around 10 s.

2 Preliminary

2.1 Blockchain

Blockchain excels in tamper-resistance and consistency, it is characterized by the fact that transactions never leave the chain. Consequently, individual blockchains remain isolated and independent from one another [11]. These characteristics reduce blockchain scalability and lead to a lack of interoperability. Connecting different blockchains to one another is called cross-chain, and Chainlink is one of the technologies that enables this.

2.2 Smart Contracts

Smart contracts are programs that exist directly on a blockchain. In Ethereum, a smart contract is an application that runs on the EVM, and it is deployed and executed via transactions. Since the state of a smart contract changes only through transactions, transactions can be completed automatically without third-party intervention, providing high reliability. Furthermore, since smart contracts reside on the blockchain, the details of transactions are recorded on the ledger and are verifiable by anyone. As a result, transactions conducted via smart contracts possess high transparency. Furthermore, Omote [10] proposed a method for generating digital signatures using smart contracts on the blockchain.

3 Related Work

In this section, we introduce related work concerning the application of blockchain in traceability, and finally, we describe the objectives of this study.

3.1 Research on Supply Chains

Problems with Supply Chain Systems That Do Not Utilize Blockchain. Traditional supply chain systems primarily utilize technologies such as barcodes and RFID. These technologies are mainly applied to supply chain systems built according to specific corporate requirements. Since these supply chain systems have different requirements and standards depending on the region or industry, the interoperability of systems between different stakeholders may decrease [6]. Furthermore, it has been pointed out that the lack of data standardization within the supply chain leads to increased time and costs for data processing and exchange [15].

Discussions on the Agri-Food Supply Chain. Niccolò et al. [12] discussed a case study regarding agricultural and food supply chain traceability using blockchain. In this study, four case studies were introduced; through their analysis, the authors examined the case of wine and pointed out that only certain phases were tracked, despite the presence of blends from various producers. Furthermore, it is pointed out that the lack of common standards among currently available blockchain case studies makes it difficult to systematically apply these findings to other cases or industries [3].

Discussions on the Seafood Supply Chain. Blaha et al. [2] focused on the fact that fish and fish products are the most traded food items globally and discussed the application of blockchain to supply chain systems for the fishing industry. In the study, they pointed out that the value chains for fisheries and aquaculture differ depending on the species of fish, the country, and the specific region. They also introduced the fact that no single, universal blockchain platform exists, but rather multiple platforms are currently in operation. This indicates that multiple independent platforms exist, leading to a lack of interoperability. They pointed out that blockchain interoperability remains a significant challenge for practical implementation.

Challenges in Blockchain Adoption. Domestichas et al. [4] conducted a discussion regarding the applicability of blockchain technology within food supply chain systems. In that study, they noted that the agri-food supply chain is reluctant to adopt blockchain due to its structural characteristics: extensive geographical dispersion and multi-stage processing. These factors make data tracking and interoperability particularly difficult. Furthermore, they pointed out that differences in business models and disparities in technical expertise among the stakeholders involved constitute significant obstacles to the consistent implementation and operation of these systems.

Additionally, Pearson et al. [13] pointed out that while blockchain is effective for improving traceability in food supply chains, it faces significant challenges regarding scalability. They estimated the projected volume of data generated in the UK over a single year and highlighted the potential scalability challenges inherent in blockchain-based supply chain systems. Furthermore, Reiblmaier et al. [17] introduced an architecture designed to address these scalability issues. Furthermore, they emphasized the necessity for these architectures to be interoperable, highlighting the need for further research to optimize scalability while maintaining the interoperability of food blockchain architectures.

3.2 Research on Cross-Chain Technology

Light Client-Based Cross-Chain. Light client-based cross-chain methods are schemes that cryptographically guarantee the validity of states on other chains by verifying the block headers and consensus proofs of the target blockchain. This method is systematized as one of the primary approaches to blockchain interoperability, utilizing a structure that employs light clients to verify the consensus state and inclusion proofs of the target chain [1]. While providing high security, this method entails significant computational costs for block header and consensus signature verification, as well as high implementation complexity.

Oracle-Based Model. The oracle-based model is a method for supplying information to a blockchain by bringing in external data through intermediaries, and is characterized by its inherent introduction of trust assumptions regarding external entities. For instance, Town Crier [5] proposes a framework that utilizes a Trusted Execution Environment (TEE) as a foundation of trust to retrieve external HTTPS data and supply it to smart contracts. Furthermore, research on decentralized oracle systems has systematically organized designs that distribute trust through consensus among multiple nodes and reputation mechanisms [8]; however, these systems still rely on certain trust assumptions regarding the oracle nodes and data sources.

Optimistic Bridge. Optimistic Bridge is a method that optimistically accept cross-chain messages or state updates, finalizing them only if no fraud is proven within a specified period. This design is systematized in research on trust-minimized optimistic verification-based Cross-Rollup Message Bridges and employs a framework that reverts states via fraud proofs in the event of malicious activity [7]. In recent bridge design research, architectures have also been proposed that ensure security through economic collateral and challenge mechanisms [14].

Our proposed method is similar in that it does not trust intermediaries and induces honesty through economic incentives; however, it is fundamentally different in that while Optimistic Bridges primarily target the validity of state transitions or asset transfers, our method targets the integrity of history based on product serial numbers and the integration of those histories.

Stateless Signature Verification Method. Stateless signature verification methods, which verify signatures generated off-chain on a smart contract, have been widely utilized in recent decentralized applications. In this context, "stateles" refers to a verification method that determines validity solely based on the message and signature being verified, without relying on other blockchain states or historical information. In Ethereum, transactions are defined as ECDSA-signed instructions, and sender verification based on these signatures is stipulated as a specification [18]. In such schemes, signature verification guarantees the authenticity of a single message, but the consistency of the entire history or the detection of missing data is not within the scope of the design.

In contrast, our proposed method uses signature verification as the root of trust and is characterized by its ability to detect missing history based on serial numbers assigned to product information, thereby ensuring historical integrity.

3.3 Limitations of Related Work

While there are numerous advantages to utilizing blockchain for supply chain systems, as discussed in Sect. 3.1, the range of products is highly diverse, the scope of traceability varies widely, and the capacity and extent to which traceability can be implemented differ across countries and regions. Furthermore, related work has demonstrated the difficulty of covering the entire scope of traceability using only a single blockchain. While blockchain-based traceability systems have been proposed, systems based on a single blockchain still suffer from a lack of interoperability.

Although many cross-chain technologies have been proposed, they remain insufficient for improving traceability in supply chain systems, particularly regarding computational complexity and the verification of consistency across the entire history of product information. While our previous research [9] utilizes multiple blockchains, Chainlink is a highly sophisticated cross-chain platform that requires significant computational costs.

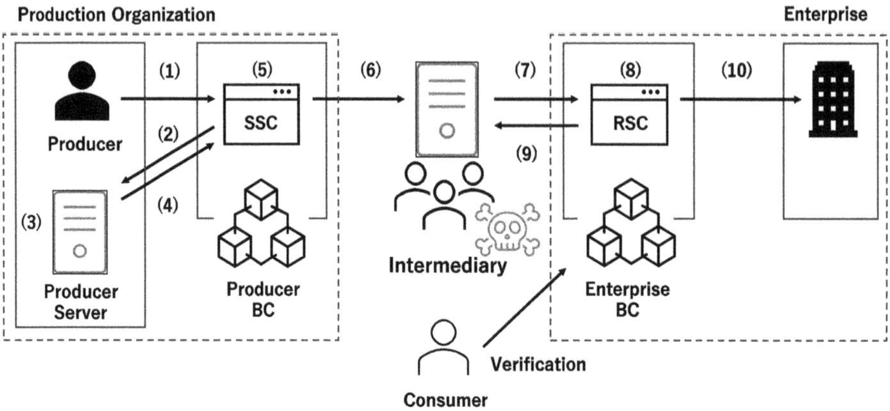

Fig. 1. Overview

4 Proposed Method

4.1 Overview

In this study, to ensure information consistency while maintaining low-cost data exchange in blockchain-based supply chains, we propose a system that implements smart contracts on both the sending and receiving blockchains to transfer and verify product information between them. The sending-side smart contract handles the disclosure of product information, while the receiving-side smart contract performs on-chain verification of that information. As a result, consumers can confirm product information simply by verifying the enterprise blockchain, eliminating the need for complex multi-chain navigation. Furthermore, we define an intermediary as the entity responsible for transferring information between blockchains. This intermediary is part of an unspecified large group and is trustless.

Furthermore, by assigning sequence numbers to each lot of the product information, the receiving-side smart contract verifies the consistency of the entire history of that information. Consequently, the consistency of product information can be maintained without relying on the trustworthiness of the unspecified intermediaries.

4.2 Components

We will now describe the components comprising this study.

- Producer: The producer is an individual or organization that produces the item (e.g., agricultural products) serving as the starting point of the product life cycle. Each producer maintains their own permissionless blockchain, where they store the producer's identity, the production location, and the production timestamp as the initial product information.
- Producer Server: The producer server retrieves the product information stored on the producer's blockchain and generates a digital signature. This signature is created using the producer server's private key, and the resulting signature is then disclosed via the SSC on the producer's blockchain (Producer BC).
- Sending Smart Contract (SSC): The SSC verifies the generated signature on-chain. Upon successful verification, it publicly discloses the product information, the signature, and the destination address.
- Enterprise: The enterprise manages the overall distribution of products and maintains a permissionless blockchain (Enterprise BC) for managing product information. This product information encompasses the final production details, processing records, and logistical history of how the product was transported; consumers can access this information by connecting to this blockchain. Furthermore, the enterprise sends production instructions to the producers.
- Receiving Smart Contract (RSC): The RSC verifies the product information and signature received from the intermediary using the producer server's public key. Product information is stored on-chain only if the verification is successful. The contract automatically executes an incentive payment to the first intermediary who successfully submits a valid signature.
- Intermediary: Intermediaries are an unspecified large group of entities that facilitate the exchange of information. They download the production information and the corresponding signature from the producer's blockchain. They issue a transaction to copy the downloaded information to the enterprise blockchain. Intermediaries use their own private keys solely for issuing the verification transaction to the RSC.
- Consumer: The consumer obtains product traceability information by accessing the public blockchain maintained by the enterprise.

4.3 Attack Model

Regarding the threat model for the proposed system, we consider the following types of attackers. It is assumed that attacks are carried out by third parties hostile to the enterprise, while the producers and the enterprise are considered trustworthy.

- Falsification of Information Between Blockchains: An attacker monitors the information being transferred between blockchains and attempts to falsify

product information by submitting fraudulent data to the Receiving Smart Contract (RSC).
- Malicious Intermediaries: A malicious intermediary issues fraudulent transactions. Furthermore, an intermediary may fail to transfer all the information to the enterprise blockchain, resulting in data omissions.

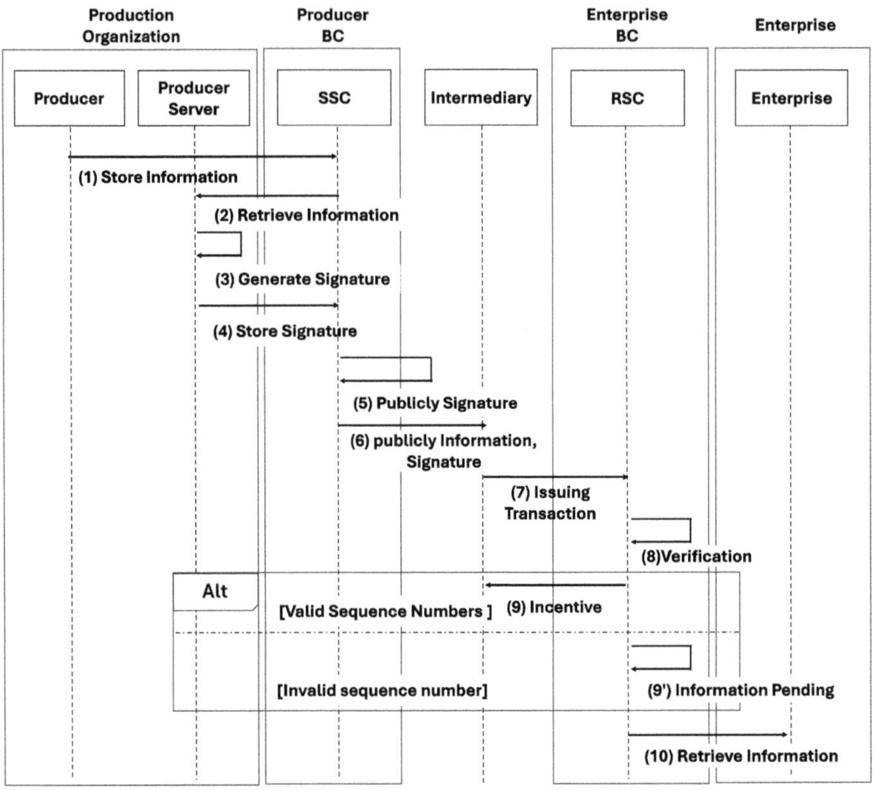

Fig. 2. Sequence Diagram

4.4 System Flow

We propose a supply chain system that connects multiple blockchains via intermediaries and enables the storage of product information, including sequence numbers. The overall architecture is illustrated in Fig. 1, and the sequence diagram is shown in Fig. 2. The system flow is as follows.

1. The producer stores the product information, which includes a sequence number, onto their own blockchain.

2. The producer server retrieves the product information from the blockchain.
3. The producer server generates a digital signature for the product information. Given the product information as M, the producer server hashes it using keccak256. An Ethereum-standard prefix is then added, and the result is hashed again with keccak256 to obtain h'. In this context, M is hashed twice to securely hash arbitrary data based on EIP-191. Finally, the signature σ is generated using the sign_message() function from the eth_account library along with the server's own private key.
4. The generated signature is stored on the producer blockchain.
5. The SSC verifies the generated signature on-chain and publicly discloses the product information, the signature, and the destination address.
6. The intermediary downloads the product information, the signature, and the destination address from the SSC.
7. The intermediary uses their own private key to issue a transaction that executes the verification process within the RSC.
8. The RSC on the enterprise blockchain verifies the signature. The RSC deployed on the blockchain receives M and σ from the intermediary. The RSC hashes M using keccak256. An Ethereum-standard prefix is added, and it is hashed again with keccak256 to obtain h''. The signature is split into r, s, v using a helper function. Here, r is the X-coordinate of the public key on the elliptic curve, where s is the proof calculated from the message hash, the private key, and the value used during the generation of r, and v indicates the sign of the Y-coordinate at the X-coordinate of the elliptic curve. The signing address ${sig_{Addr}}'$ is derived from h'', r, s, v using the ecrecover() function. This derived address is compared with the producer server's signing address sig_{Addr}, and if they match, M is stored on the blockchain.
9. The RSC verifies the sequence number stored on the enterprise blockchain and automatically pays an incentive to the intermediary who was the first to submit a valid signature.
10. The enterprise retrieves the product information from the enterprise blockchain.

5 Implementation Evaluation

In order to demonstrate the feasibility of the proposed method, on-chain signature verification is performed to facilitate the exchange of information between different blockchains.

5.1 Environment

To demonstrate the feasibility of the proposed method across different blockchain environments, we selected the Sepolia testnet (an Ethereum testnet) and the XDC Apothem net (testnet environment for XDC) as the platforms for performing on-chain signature verification. Additionally, a Python program was employed to act as the intermediary, utilizing the Web3.py library to monitor events and issue the necessary transactions.

5.2 Implementation Details

We implemented a smart contract on the blockchain that verifies the product information received from Python. A smart contract has the following functions:

- getEthSignedMessageHash(): This is a function that generates the Ethereum signing hash h'' from the product information message M received from the intermediary.
- splitSignature(): This is an auxiliary function to split the signature σ, received from the intermediary for the product information, into r, s, v and recover the signing address.
- verify(): This is a function that verifies the validity of a signature using Solidity's 'ecrecover()' function, based on the registered public key and the values h'', r, s, v obtained from the two auxiliary functions: getEthSignedMessageHash() and splitSignature().
- addKey(): This is a function for the enterprise to register the producer's public key within the smart contract.
- removeKey(): This is a function to delete the public key registered in the smart contract.
- contains(): This is an auxiliary function to determine whether the public key contained within the message received from the intermediary is registered in the smart contract.

In addition, we implemented a Python program to serve as an intermediary. The Python program has the following features:

- Transaction Signature: The intermediary generates a transaction to execute the smart contract using their own private key. This transaction includes the message M and the signature σ downloaded from the source blockchain.

5.3 Experimental Procedure

(i) A signature is generated for the text data using the eth_account library in Python.
(ii) Using the Web3.py library, a transaction is calculated to send the generated signature to the smart contracts on the Sepolia and XDC Apothem chains.
(iii) The smart contract deployed on the blockchain verifies the text data and signature received from the Python program by utilizing the recovered signing address.
(iv) If the verification is successful, the text data is recorded on the blockchain.
(v) We will measure the gas cost and the time required from the moment the transaction is sent until the verification is successful and the text data is recorded on the blockchain.

5.4 Measurement of Gas Costs

We sent 20-byte and 200-byte text messages from the Python program to the smart contract and measured the gas costs required for the on-chain verification. Measurements were conducted ten times for both Sepolia and Apothem, and the average gas cost was calculated. The results are shown in Table 1. Additionally, we measured the gas costs while varying the number of producers among 1, 20, 40, 60, 80, and 100. These results are presented in Fig. 3.

Table 1. Transaction Gas Cost

Target chain	20 bytes	200 bytes
Sepolia	0.0014 Eth	0.0021 Eth
Apothem	0.0018 XDC	0.0029 XDC

Table 2. Verification time

Target chain	20 bytes	200 bytes
Sepolia	11.4545 sec	9.9295 sec
Apothem	3.1030 sec	2.7277 sec

5.5 Measurement of Verification Time

We sent 20-byte and 200-byte text messages from the Python program to the smart contract and measured the time required for the on-chain verification to be completed. Measurements were conducted ten times for both Sepolia and XDC Apothem, and the average verification time was calculated. The results are shown in Table 2. Additionally, measurements were conducted for the verification time while varying the number of producers among 1, 20, 40, 60, 80, and 100. The results are shown in Fig. 4.

6 Discussion

6.1 Consistency Assurance

Consistency of information is critical in traceability. In the proposed method, information is transferred outside the blockchain when exchanging data between two blockchains. However, due to ECDSA signatures, falsification is difficult. Furthermore, since the intermediary does not generate the signature for the product information M, this system is secure against the leakage of the intermediary's private key.

6.2 Gas Cost

From the experimental results, the gas cost for transaction verification was approximately 0.002 tokens for both Sepolia and Apothem when comparing token amounts (as of February 2026, 1 ETH is approximately $2,004.23 and 1 XDC is approximately $0.03). The gas cost for Apothem was approximately 1/77,000 of that for Sepolia. These costs have been significantly reduced compared to our previous research. Furthermore, the gas cost remained almost constant regardless of the text data size. This is likely because Ethereum's electronic signature process involves hashing the product information M before signing, which ensures that the signature length remains unchanged. Furthermore, the gas cost increases linearly with the number of public keys for both Sepolia and XDC Apothem.

6.3 Verification Time

Based on the experimental results in Table 2, when the target chain was Sepolia, the average time was 11.4545 s for 20-byte text data and 9.9295 s for 200-byte text data. In the case of public blockchains, verification time depends on the degree of network congestion. For this reason, it is considered that the time for 200-byte data was shorter regardless of the text data size. Additionally, when the target chain was Apothem, the average time was 3.1030 s for 20-byte text data and 2.7277 s for 200-byte text data.

Apothem employs XDPoS (XDC Delegated Proof of Stake) as its consensus algorithm. This is an algorithm in which master nodes, elected as representatives, take turns generating blocks. As a result, transactions are processed more rapidly compared to Sepolia, where blocks are generated by a large number of validators.

In both cases, the verification time remained constant relative to the size of the text data. These verification times have been significantly reduced compared

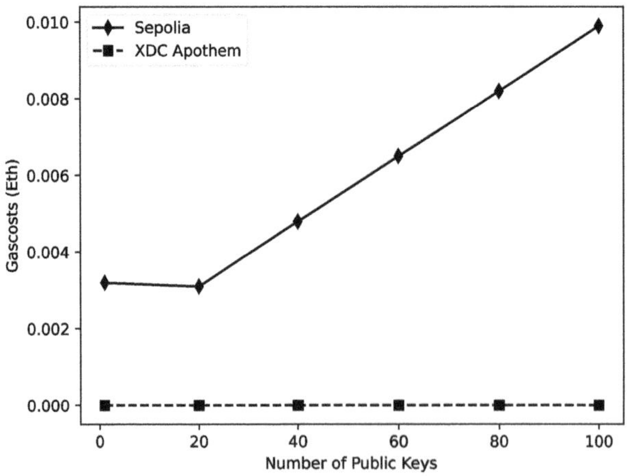

Fig. 3. Gas cost vs. Number of public keys

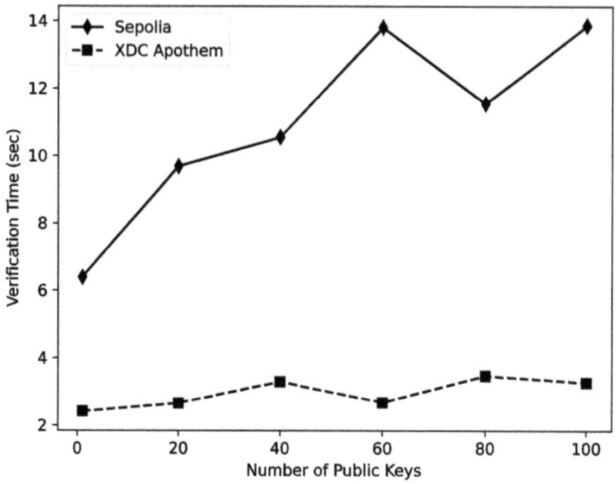

Fig. 4. Verification time vs. Number of public keys

to our previous research. Furthermore, while the verification time for Sepolia tended to increase with the number of public keys, it remained nearly constant for XDC Apothem.

6.4 Tampering of Information Between Blockchains

The receiving smart contract implemented on the enterprise blockchain receives product information and a signature from the transaction provided by the intermediary. At this point, the smart contract hashes the product information and directly verifies the signature. Consequently, the intermediary cannot pass the verification with counterfeit product information. Furthermore, the intermediary uses their own private key only for issuing verification transactions to the RSC. Since the electronic signatures for product information are stored on the producer's server and do not depend on the intermediary, the system allows for an unspecified number of intermediaries who do not require a high level of trust. Additionally, since smart contracts store information on the blockchain, tampering with data after cross-chain transmission is difficult. Therefore, this system prevents the content written by producers and enterprise from being altered, thereby maintaining the integrity of the traceability.

6.5 Missing Information

When generating signatures within the production organization, a sequence number is assigned to the information to be disclosed. By verifying these sequence numbers at the RSC (Receiving Smart Contract) within the enterprise blockchain, the system can prevent information from being missing.

6.6 Limitations

The proposed method ensures the consistency of product information through signature verification using smart contracts. While smart contracts can be implemented on many blockchains, they cannot be used on the most well-known chain, Bitcoin.

Furthermore, the proposed method assumes that product information is disclosed without encryption. While storing unencrypted information on the blockchain is necessary for consumers to verify the product data correctly, there is a need for further discussion regarding whether all product information should be fully disclosed.

7 Conclusion

In this study, we proposed, implemented, and evaluated a third party independent supply chain system that utilizes multiple blockchains. We implemented smart contracts on both the Sepolia and XDC Apothem chains and demonstrated that information can be exchanged without relying on the trustworthiness of intermediaries. Furthermore, we measured the gas costs and time required for transaction verification, demonstrating that the proposed method is practical. This research succeeded in significantly reducing both gas costs and verification time compared to our previously proposed method utilizing Chainlink. Additionally, by assigning sequence numbers to product information, the system can prevent information loss caused by malicious intermediaries. This has effectively lowered the barrier to utilizing blockchain technology within supply chain systems.

Acknowledgments. This work was supported by JSPS KAKENHI Grant Number JP25H01106.

References

1. Belchior, R., Vasconcelos, A., Guerreiro, S., Correia, M.: A survey on blockchain interoperability: past, present, and future trends. ACM Comput. Surv. (CSUR) **54**(8), 1–41 (2021)
2. Blaha, F.: Blockchain application in seafood value chains. In: FAO Fisheries and Aquaculture Circular, vol. 1207 (2020). https://api.semanticscholar.org/CorpusID:241391702
3. Clohessy, T., Acton, T., Rogers, N.: Blockchain adoption: technological, organisational and environmental considerations. In: Treiblmaier, H., Beck, R. (eds.) Business Transformation through Blockchain, pp. 47–76. Springer, Cham (2019). https://doi.org/10.1007/978-3-319-98911-2_2
4. Demestichas, K., Peppes, N., Alexakis, T., Adamopoulou, E.: Blockchain in agriculture traceability systems: a review. Appl. Sci. **10**(12) (2020). https://doi.org/10.3390/app10124113. https://www.mdpi.com/2076-3417/10/12/4113

5. F., Z., Cecchettiand, E., K., C., A., J., E., S.: Town crier: an authenticated data feed for smart contracts. In: Proceedings of the 2016 ACM SIGSAC Conference on Computer and Communications Security (CCS) (2016)
6. Fan, Z.P., Wu, X.Y., Cao, B.B.: Considering the traceability awareness of consumers: should the supply chain adopt the blockchain technology? Annals of. Oper. Res. 1–24 (2022)
7. Fekete, D.L., Kiss, A.: Trust-minimized optimistic cross-rollup arbitrary message bridge. J. Netw. Comput. Appl. **221**, 103771 (2024)
8. H., A.B., M., H., R., K., K., R.C.: Trustworthy blockchain oracles: review, comparison, and open research challenges. IEEE Access **8**, 85675–85685 (2020)
9. Kadosugi, A., Omote, K.: A traceability system with multiple blockchains. In: 8th International Conference on Blockchain Technology and Applications, (2025) ICBTA 2025
10. Omote, K.: Can smart contracts generate digital signatures? 7th International Conference on Blockchain Computing and Applications (BCCA 2025), pp. 24–30 (2025)
11. Ou, W., Huang, S., Zheng, J., Zhang, Q., Zeng, G., Han, W.: An overview on cross-chain: mechanism, platforms, challenges and advances. Comput. Netw. **218**, 109378 (2022). https://doi.org/10.1016/j.comnet.2022.109378. https://www.sciencedirect.com/science/article/pii/S1389128622004121
12. Patelli, N., Mandrioli, M.: Blockchain technology and traceability in the agrifood industry. J. Food Sci. **85**(11), 3670–3678 (2020)
13. Pearson, S., et al.: Are distributed ledger technologies the panacea for food traceability? Glob. Food Sec. **20**, 145–149 (2019). https://doi.org/10.1016/j.gfs.2019.02.002. https://www.sciencedirect.com/science/article/pii/S2211912418301408
14. Scaffino, G., Aumayr, L., Bastankhah, M., Avarikioti, Z., Maffei, M.: Alba: The dawn of scalable bridges for blockchains. Cryptology ePrint Archive (2024)
15. Storøy, J., Thakur, M., Olsen, P.: The tracefood framework – principles and guidelines for implementing traceability in food value chains. J. Food Eng. **115**(1), 41–48 (2013). https://doi.org/10.1016/j.jfoodeng.2012.09.018. https://www.sciencedirect.com/science/article/pii/S0260877412004529
16. Tian, F.: An agri-food supply chain traceability system for China based on RFID & blockchain technology. In: 2016 13th International Conference on Service Systems and Service Management (ICSSSM), pp. 1–6 (2016). https://doi.org/10.1109/ICSSSM.2016.7538424
17. Tian, F.: A supply chain traceability system for food safety based on HACCP, blockchain & internet of things. In: 2017 International Conference on Service Systems and Service Management, pp. 1–6 (2017). https://doi.org/10.1109/ICSSSM.2017.7996119
18. Wood, G., et al.: Ethereum: a secure decentralised generalised transaction ledger. Ethereum Project Yellow Paper **151**(2014), 1–32 (2014)
19. Yu, H., Nikolić, I., Hou, R., Saxena, P.: Ohie: blockchain scaling made simple. In: 2020 IEEE Symposium on Security and Privacy (SP), pp. 90–105 (2020). https://doi.org/10.1109/SP40000.2020.00008

A Fiat-Anchored Dual-Rail Triple-Entry Architecture for SSC-Based K-12 Financial Systems

Minh Tuan Le[1,2], Dat Thanh Pham[3](✉), and Congdu Nguyen[4,5]

[1] Department of Electrical and Electronic Engineering, Hanoi Open University, Hanoi, Vietnam
lmtuan@hou.edu.vn
[2] KOET Co., Ltd, Ho Chi Minh City, Vietnam
[3] School of Computing, Phenikaa University, Hanoi, Vietnam
dat.phamthanh1@phenikaa-uni.edu.vn
[4] Green House Culture JSC, Ho Chi Minh City, Vietnam
du.nguyen@thessc.vn
[5] Faculty of Information Technology, Dong Do University, Hanoi, Vietnam

Abstract. School Services Center (SSC) platforms increasingly support tuition and fee collection across multiple educational institutions, yet they often face a persistent separation between fiat settlement and cross-party payment-state visibility, leading to reconciliation delays and weak shared auditability. This paper is grounded in an existing SSC business system and proposes a fiat-anchored dual-rail architecture in which regulated fiat settlement remains off-chain, while payment evidence is normalized, batched into Merkle commitments, and anchored on Cardano as a tamper-evident third entry. In this design, blockchain is not used as the payment rail; instead, it functions as a public evidentiary layer that supports independent verification without exposing raw financial payloads. We evaluate a full-stack prototype using 10,000 synthetic payment events and report a maximum batch size of 1,681 events per anchoring transaction, 609 ms submission-to-receipt latency, 0.0735 ms local proof verification, and an estimated monthly anchoring cost of approximately $4.28 USD under the evaluated workload assumptions. These results indicate promising operational feasibility for extending real SSC deployments with publicly verifiable reconciliation evidence while preserving fiat-native compliance.

Keywords: Triple-entry accounting · Cardano · K-12 finance · SSC · blockchain reconciliation

1 Introduction

School Services Center (SSC) platforms play an increasingly important role in coordinating tuition and fee collection across multiple educational institutions. In

S. Chen et al. (Eds.): METAVERSE 2026, LNCS 16963, pp. 90–98, 2027.
https://doi.org/10.1007/978-3-032-36773-0_7

this study, we focus on an existing SSC business system that already supports real payment processing and operational school-facing workflows [1]. In such settings, the main operational friction is often not how fiat money moves, but how payment-status information propagates across the SSC platform, school systems, and parent-facing interfaces. While funds settle through regulated banking channels, the corresponding status information frequently arrives through asynchronous callbacks, delayed reconciliation files, or heterogeneous wallet notifications. This mismatch forces SSC platforms to maintain centralized operational databases that function as local truths, but not as independently verifiable shared truths across organizational boundaries.

A natural temptation is to use blockchain as a direct payment rail. However, in K-12 financial settings, tuition and fee settlement must remain fiat-native and compliant with existing regulatory and banking constraints. The practical challenge is therefore narrower and more realistic: how to create a shared, tamper-evident evidentiary layer around off-chain settlement events without replacing the regulated payment infrastructure of an already deployed SSC system.

This paper addresses that challenge by proposing a *fiat-anchored dual-rail triple-entry architecture*. The key idea is to separate the *Value Layer*, where fiat transfer and banking settlement remain unchanged, from the *Information Layer*, where normalized payment evidence is batched and anchored on a public blockchain. In this way, blockchain is used as a verification and auditability substrate rather than as a monetary settlement mechanism.

This study addresses the gap between legacy fiat processing and cryptographically verifiable state synchronization. Our contributions are explicitly architectural and empirical:

1. We formalize the payment mismatch problem not as a failure of payment rails, but as the absence of an independently verifiable evidentiary layer in operational, compliance-bound educational systems.
2. We introduce a domain-specific architectural pattern (a fiat-anchored dual-rail triple-entry model) that strictly isolates the regulated Value Layer from a publicly anchored Information Layer using Merkle batching on Cardano.
3. We evaluate a full-stack prototype, demonstrating the operational feasibility, verification efficiency, and cost-predictability of this architectural configuration under representative SSC workloads.

2 Problem Setting and Related Work

Figure 1 summarizes the legacy SSC financial architecture. Parents initiate payments through heterogeneous channels. Funds move into SSC collection accounts, while information traverses an ingestion layer, a central store, and finally school systems. This architecture suffers from incomplete event capture, manual exception handling, and delayed synchronization. A reconciliation fault occurs when visible invoice state diverges across systems:

$$\exists i \in I,\ \exists k_1 \neq k_2 : S_{k_1}(i) \neq S_{k_2}(i).$$

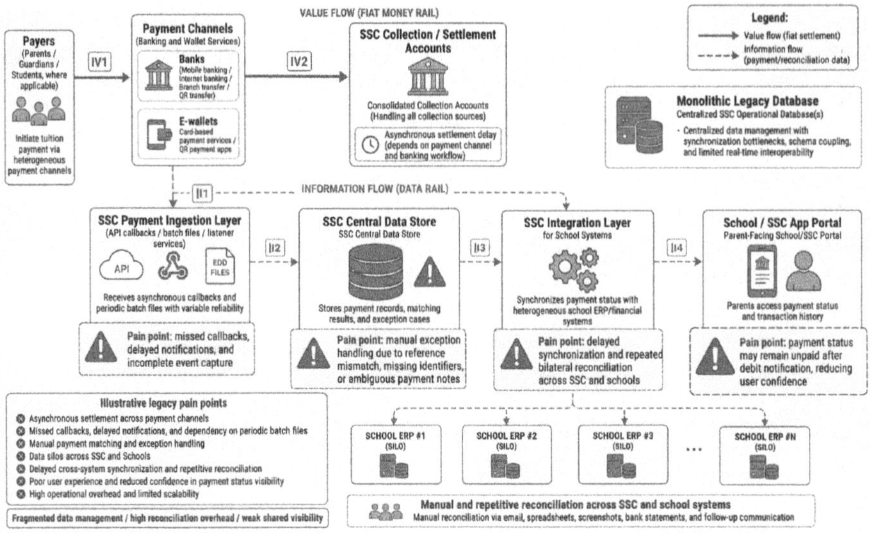

Fig. 1. Legacy SSC financial architecture for K-12 payment processing, illustrating the fragmentation between fiat value flow and reconciliation information flow.

The problem considered here is not the creation of an SSC platform from scratch. Rather, we establish a domain-specific architectural pattern for SSC-based financial reconciliation. This pattern enhances existing deployments with a stronger evidentiary layer that ensures auditability and cross-party state consistency without disrupting regulated workflows [1]. This distinction is important because the proposed architecture must coexist with real fiat workflows, regulated payment operations, and existing user-facing services rather than replace them.

The proposed architecture sits at the intersection of triple-entry accounting (TEA) and blockchain-based reconciliation [6]. Grigg describes the third entry as a cryptographically verifiable shared receipt across organizational boundaries [2,7]. More recently, survey work on blockchain-based TEA in B2B contexts has shown that the field is still evolving, with many studies remaining conceptual or focused on high-level accounting transformation rather than deployable reconciliation workflows [3,4]. In that sense, TEA is best understood not merely as an accounting metaphor, but as a design pattern for producing independently verifiable transaction evidence among partially trusted parties [5,6].

This perspective is especially relevant in payment reconciliation [13]. In SSC settings, the dominant pain point is not the absence of a payment rail, but the absence of a shared evidentiary layer that can survive asynchronous notifications, local database updates, and cross-system inconsistency. Existing centralized solutions can synchronize state, but they do not inherently provide public tamper-evidence or independent third-party verification [8]. Conversely, crypto-native payment architectures often assume that value transfer and proof generation occur on the same rail, which does not fit regulated K-12 tuition processing.

Our work therefore targets a narrower and more operationally grounded gap: *off-chain fiat settlement with on-chain evidentiary anchoring* for an existing SSC business context. Rather than moving tuition payments onto a blockchain, we anchor only canonicalized payment evidence through batched commitments [5]. Cardano's extended UTXO (eUTXO) model is appropriate in this context because it supports deterministic transaction semantics for discrete evidence commitments [9,10,14], while CIP-20 metadata provides a lightweight mechanism to attach Merkle-root references to on-chain records [11].

To clarify the architectural positioning of our proposed system against existing paradigms, Table 1 delineates the boundaries between centralized SSC logs, generic Triple-Entry Accounting (TEA) concepts, and our domain-specific dual-rail approach. While traditional TEA conceptualizes shared verification, our architecture uniquely configures these primitives to satisfy the stringent compliance requirement of preserving fiat-native settlement.

Table 1. Architectural positioning against existing paradigms

Dimension	Centralized-Log	Generic-TEA	Proposed Dual-Rail
Monetary Settlement	Fiat-native	Often on-chain	**Fiat-native (Off-chain)**
Reconciliation	Local database	Shared ledger	**Anchored Merkle roots**
Verification	Requires trust	Shared access	**Independent (Third-entry)**
Data Privacy	Access control	Often public	**Off-chain raw payloads**
Primary Context	Operational	Conceptual	**K-12 Compliance-bound**

3 Proposed Architecture

The system is logically divided into two independent rails to balance compliance with transparency, as detailed in Fig. 2. The *Value Layer* preserves the existing regulated banking and payment infrastructure already used by the SSC platform. The *Information Layer* captures notifications, matches them to invoices, and anchors commitments to a public eUTXO blockchain. This separation avoids disruption to compliant fiat processing while still creating a verifiable evidentiary trail.

3.1 Ingestion and Anchoring Pipeline

Event capture is managed by an *SSC-authorized oracle gateway* that applies timestamping, deduplication, and idempotent ingestion controls. The platform normalizes heterogeneous bank and wallet payloads into a canonical evidence format and aggregates them into Merkle-tree batches. Batching is a critical design

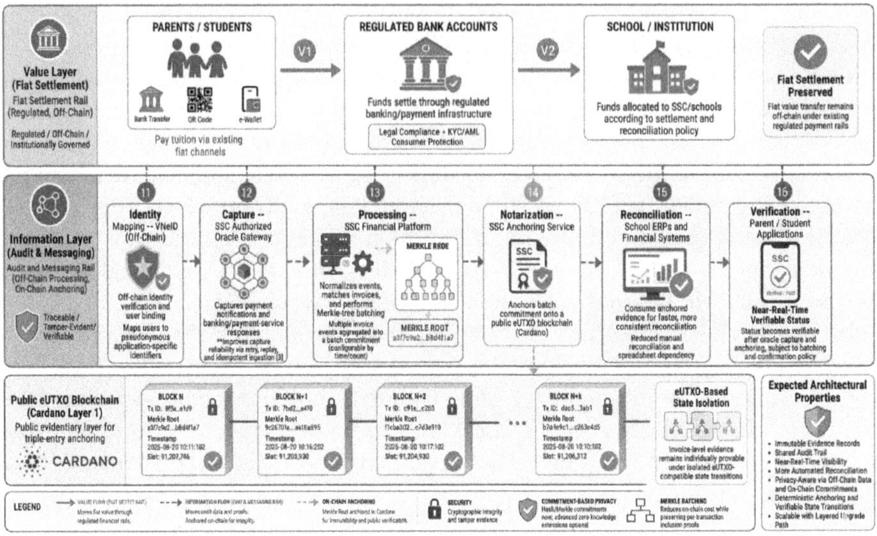

Fig. 2. Proposed blockchain-integrated SSC architecture. Fiat value remains off-chain, while payment evidence is processed off-chain and anchored on-chain for verification.

choice for public-chain viability because it reduces both operational cost and privacy exposure compared with publishing full payloads or broadcasting one on-chain transaction per payment event [5].

The SSC anchoring service subsequently submits the batch commitment, i.e., the Merkle root, to the Cardano Layer 1 network using CIP-20 standardized transaction metadata [11]. Identity mapping is envisioned to be handled off-chain via conceptual VNeID-linked institutional workflows to avoid exposing sensitive student or payer information on-chain [12]. The blockchain record therefore serves as a public commitment to inclusion and order, while sensitive business data remains under compliant off-chain control.

3.2 Triple-Entry Interpretation

In our context, triple-entry accounting is defined precisely as follows [7]. Entry 1 is the collector-side record maintained by the SSC. Entry 2 is the obligation-side record maintained by the school or institutional counterparty. Entry 3 is the cryptographically verifiable shared receipt derived from the anchored commitment and the corresponding Merkle proof [13]. This third entry does not replace institutional ledgers, instead, it narrows the trust boundary by giving all authorized parties a common verification reference for event inclusion and chronological consistency [7,13].

3.3 Trust Assumptions and Threat Model

We assume that regulated fiat transfer, banking finality, and legal settlement remain external to the proposed system. The SSC platform is responsible for event capture, normalization, batching, anchoring, and proof distribution. Under this model, the architecture is designed to mitigate several practical risks: post-hoc modification of payment-status records, inconsistent invoice visibility across parties, duplicate callback ingestion, malformed event submission, and repudiation of whether a payment event was included in a committed batch.

At the same time, the architecture does not guarantee that an upstream payment message is semantically correct before canonicalization. It also does not eliminate governance risk if an authorized operator intentionally omits a valid event prior to anchoring. These limitations are important because the proposed design strengthens evidence integrity and verifiability, but it does not replace institutional controls for operational correctness, authorization, or dispute resolution [8]. To mitigate selective omission prior to anchoring, future production deployments must enforce multi-signature approval among independent SSC operators or publish pre-commitment batch hashes to an external public bulletin board.

4 Experimental Results and Discussion

To empirically validate the architecture's operational viability, we developed a full-stack prototype aligned with the workflow assumptions of the existing SSC platform [1]. The ingestion layer was implemented in Python/FastAPI and evaluated over a dataset of 10,000 synthetic payment events (simulating a uniform temporal distribution of full tuition payments with an average 256-byte JSON payload per event). The anchoring service was implemented in Node.js using Mesh SDK and connected to the Cardano Preprod testnet through the Koios API. All source code, evaluation scripts, and reproducible datasets are available at https://github.com/tuanle-max/SSC-DualRail-TEA.

Table 2 summarizes the main performance, reliability, and operating-cost metrics. We report the metrics as prototype observations rather than production guarantees because the current evaluation uses synthetic event streams and a testnet environment, even though the design objective is grounded in a real SSC deployment context.

The 609 ms latency (LAT-1) reflects the API submission-to-receipt response time. On Mainnet, network congestion and mempool dynamics may delay final on-chain inclusion by 1–2 block cycles ($\sim$ 20 to 40 s), though off-chain acknowledgment remains near-instantaneous. The measured 0.0735 ms proof verification time (VER-1, evaluated on a standard Intel Core i7, 16GB RAM environment) also suggests that schools or auditors can validate inclusion using standard client environments without operating full nodes.

To test ingestion robustness, we injected malformed events at a rate of 15.70% (FIR-1). The gateway successfully isolated these malformed entries before the batching phase, which supports the use of canonicalization and validation as

Table 2. Experimental metrics of the SSC-DualRail-TEA prototype.

Metric ID	Value	Definition and Context
LAT-1 (Latency)	609 ms	Submission-to-receipt latency (API response time before block confirmation)
BATCH-1 (Batch Size)	1,681 items	Payment evidence events anchored per Merkle root
FIR-1 (Fault Rate)	15.70%	Fault injection rate in simulated stress-test scenario
VER-1 (Verification)	0.0735 ms	Local Merkle-proof validation time on client side
COST-1 (OpEx)	\$4.28 USD/mo	Anchoring cost estimate (15.30 ADA/mo at approx. \$0.28/ADA)

a protective boundary between heterogeneous external notifications and the anchoring layer. By aggregating up to 1,681 payment events per commitment (BATCH-1) - the empirical maximum before exceeding Cardano's 16 KB CIP-20 metadata limit - the prototype demonstrates optimal cost predictability. Smaller batch sizes (e.g., 100 or 500) yield proportionally lower latency but linearly increase the per-event anchoring cost. Assuming a medium-scale SSC workload of 5,000 invoices per day, the monthly anchoring cost is strictly bounded at approximately 15.30 ADA. Under varying market conditions, this translates linearly to \$1.53 at \$0.10/ADA, \$4.28 at \$0.28/ADA, and \$15.30 at \$1.00/ADA. While this estimate is encouraging, it remains sensitive to transaction frequency and metadata size. The current study therefore supports the claim of *practical feasibility under prototype conditions*, rather than full production readiness.

4.1 Limitations

This evaluation has several limitations. First, the workload is synthetic and may not capture the full heterogeneity and burstiness of production SSC traffic. Second, operating on Cardano Preprod limits external validity for throughput and finality behavior. Third, compared to a one-payment-per-transaction baseline on Cardano (which would require 1,681 transactions for a full batch), our batching approach reduces on-chain fee overhead by approximately 99.94%, validating its cost-effectiveness over naive implementations. Fourth, while the current design reduces tampering risk after evidence creation, it does not inherently prevent selective omission before anchoring. Finally, off-chain data availability remains critical; loss of the local SSC database prevents Merkle proof reconstruction, even though the on-chain root remains immutable.

5 Conclusion

This paper presented a blockchain-integrated architecture for SSC-based K-12 financial systems using a fiat-anchored dual-rail triple-entry model. The design preserves regulated fiat settlement while introducing a public evidentiary layer for tamper-evident reconciliation. A functional Cardano-based prototype showed that payment evidence can be batched efficiently, verified locally with negligible latency, and anchored at low monthly operating cost under the evaluated assumptions.

Taken together, the results indicate promising operational feasibility for extending real SSC deployments in which compliance requirements make fiat-native settlement non-negotiable. More broadly, the study suggests that public blockchain infrastructure can add value in educational finance not by replacing payment rails, but by strengthening the integrity and verifiability of cross-party payment-state evidence. Future work will focus on production-scale workloads, omission-resistant governance mechanisms, and broader comparisons against alternative centralized reconciliation architectures.

Acknowledgments. This study was partially supported by Hanoi Open University, Phenikaa University, Dong Do University, KOET Co., Ltd and Green House Culture JSC in Vietnam.

References

1. RAR school services center: SSC tuition payment platform. https://hocphi.rar-ssc.vn/
2. Grigg, I.: Triple entry accounting. J. Risk Financ. Manag. **17**(2), 76 (2024). https://doi.org/10.3390/jrfm17020076
3. Sarwar, M.I., Nisar, K., Khan, I., Shehzad, D.: Blockchains and triple-entry accounting for B2B business models. Ledger, **8** (2023). https://doi.org/10.5195/ledger.2023.288
4. Sarwar, M.I., Khan, I., Maghrabi, L.A., Nisar, K.: a survey on blockchain-based triple-entry accounting in B2B context. J. Inf. Syst. **40**(1), 25–45 (2026). https://doi.org/10.2308/ISYS-2024-004
5. Pan, L., Vaughan, O., Wright, C.S.: A private and efficient triple-entry accounting protocol on bitcoin. J. Risk Financ. Manag. **16**(9), 400 (2023). https://doi.org/10.3390/jrfm16090400
6. Joseph, R., et al.: Triple-entry accounting (TEA) and blockchain implementation in accounting and finance – a survey. In: 2023 International Conference on Business Analytics for Technology and Security (ICBATS), Dubai, United Arab Emirates, pp. 1–7 (2023). https://doi.org/10.1109/ICBATS57792.2023.10111259
7. Ibañez, J.I., Bayer, C.N., Tasca, P., Xu, J.: Triple-entry accounting, blockchain, and next of kin: towards a standardisation of ledger terminology. In: Aggarwal, R., Tasca, P. (eds.) Digital Assets: Pricing, Allocation and Regulation, pp. 198–226. Cambridge University Press (2025)
8. Bonyuet, D.: Overview and impact of blockchain on auditing. Internat. J. Digit. Acc. Res. (2020). https://api.semanticscholar.org/CorpusID:215761398
9. Pomogalova, A.V., Martyniuk, A.A., Yesalov, K.E.: Key features and formation of transactions in the case of using UTxO, EUTxO and account based data storage models. In: 2022 International Conference on Modern Network Technologies (MoNeTec), Moscow, Russian Federation, pp. 1–7 (2022). https://doi.org/10.1109/MoNeTec55448.2022.9960753

10. Cardano developers: extended UTXO (EUTXO). https://developers.cardano.org/docs/learn/core-concepts/eutxo/. (Accessed 12 May 2026)
11. Cardano foundation: cardano improvement proposal CIP-20: transaction metadata label registry. https://cips.cardano.org/cip/CIP-0020 (Accessed 12 May 2026)
12. VNeID: official website of vietnam national electronic identification. https://vneid.com/. (Accessed 12 May 2026)
13. Faccia, A., Moşteanu, N.R., Leonardo, L.P.: Blockchain hash, the missing axis of the accounts to settle the triple entry bookkeeping system. In: Proceedings of the 2020 12th International Conference on Information Management and Engineering (ICIME 2020), pp. 18–23. Association for Computing Machinery, Amsterdam, Netherlands (2020). https://doi.org/10.1145/3430279.3430283
14. Brünjes, L., Gabbay, M.J.: UTxO- vs account-based smart contract blockchain programming paradigms. In: Margaria, T., Steffen, B. (eds.) Leveraging Applications of Formal Methods, Verification and Validation: Applications. ISoLA 2020. Lecture Notes in Computer Science, vol. 12478. Springer, Cham (2020). https://doi.org/10.1007/978-3-030-61467-6_6

Author Index

A
Aftab, Salim 17

K
Kadosugi, Aoi 75

L
Le, Minh Tuan 90
Liao, Hailong 46
Liu, Jingwen 60

N
Nguyen, Congdu 90

O
Okutsu, Kousei 1
Omote, Kazumasa 1, 75

P
Pham, Dat Thanh 90

R
Ren, Shaofeng 60

S
Sajid, Taha 17

T
Takahashi, Taisei 1

V
Vats, Anmol 30

Y
Yao, Qintao 60

S. Chen et al. (Eds.): METAVERSE 2026, LNCS 16963, p. 99, 2027.
https://doi.org/10.1007/978-3-032-36773-0

GPSR Compliance
The European Union's (EU) General Product Safety Regulation (GPSR) is a set of rules that requires consumer products to be safe and our obligations to ensure this.

If you have any concerns about our products, you can contact us on

ProductSafety@springernature.com

In case Publisher is established outside the EU, the EU authorized representative is:

Springer Nature Customer Service Center GmbH
Europaplatz 3
69115 Heidelberg, Germany

www.ingramcontent.com/pod-product-compliance
Ingram Content Group UK Ltd.
Pitfield, Milton Keynes, MK11 3LW, UK
UKHW021239300926
15471UKWH00013B/769
* 9 7 8 3 0 3 2 3 6 7 7 2 3 *